Midlife Magic

The 7 Day Self-Care Plan to Boost Your Energy and Make You Smile

Bonnie Leonard, EdD

First Stillwater River Publications Edition

Library of Congress Control Number: 2018931933

ISBN-10: 1-946-30049-7
ISBN-13: 978-1-946-30049-2

1 2 3 4 5 6 7 8 9 10
Written by Bonnie Leonard
Published by Stillwater River Publications, Glocester, RI, USA.

Publisher's Cataloging-In-Publication Data
(Prepared by The Donohue Group, Inc.)

Names: Leonard, Bonnie.
Title: Midlife magic: the 7 day self-care plan to boost your energy & make you smile / Bonnie Leonard, EdD.
Description: First Stillwater River Publications edition. | Glocester, RI, USA : Stillwater River Publications, [2018]
Identifiers: ISBN 9781946300492 | ISBN 1946300497
Subjects: LCSH: Leonard, Bonnie. | Middle-aged persons--Psychology. | Midlife crisis. | Self-actualization (Psychology) | Self-help techniques. | Happiness.
Classification: LCC HQ1059.4 .L43 2018 | DDC 305.244--dc23

All client and student names have been altered and occasionally their attributes have been combined to protect their privacy.

For my two big-hearted sons,
Tim and Nate,
in gratitude for their ongoing love, support,
and encouragement

Contents

INTRODUCTION...1

DAY 1: Self Compassion.....................................11

DAY 2: Happy Body 27

DAY 3: Supportive Connections...........................49

DAY 4: Optimal Organization............................67

DAY 5: Nurturing Environment.........................89

DAY 6: Time on Your Terms 103

DAY 7: Completion/Celebration..................117

APPLAUSE TIME 131

Acknowledgments 136

Midlife Magic

Love yourself first, and everything else falls into line.

– Lucille Ball

INTRODUCTION

Welcome to Midlife Magic: The 7 Day Self-Care Plan to Boost Your Energy and Make You Smile—a book designed especially for women stuck at the midlife crossroads wondering what's next. Since you picked up this book, I'm guessing you may feel somewhat burnt out, unsettled, or even discontent—wanting to move forward in your life, but unsure of what step to take. You've come to the right place.

At midlife, psychological forces go to work pressuring you to grow and change. It's a time of falling apart and coming together in a new way as you become better acquainted with yourself at a deeper level. This pivotal period catapults you into a time of reflection and reevaluation, a chance to come to terms with your own mortality and seek new ground for the purpose of your life.

The secret to navigating the midlife period successfully is a deep exploration of your inner world, because there is much more inside you to be discovered, investigated, and later expressed in the outer world. Such a challenging inner quest requires energy. To find this energy you need to bring a particular kind of attention to yourself—probably a different kind of care than your daily habits would reveal right now. To set about a midlife expedition, you must become a hearty and resilient traveler. *Midlife Magic* is designed to give you that extra boost of energy and keep a smile on your face for the midlife journey.

Pretend for a moment you plan to take a cross-country road trip. Before embarking on such a journey, you would surely take your car for a comprehensive check up, approve any necessary repairs and undoubtedly leave with a full tank of gas, a map and your GPS. You might even give your vehicle a good wash, wax and polish, so you could set off on your trip in a happy state of mind.

In a similar way, you can prepare for the rigors of your own midlife odyssey by simply following the seven day program outlined in this book.

My Midlife Adventure

To begin our journey together, I invite you to travel back in time with me, when I found myself feeling distracted and unsettled on the third floor of an empty Victorian house.

Lost in reverie, I wiped a desk mindlessly over and over with the dust cloth in my hand while my thoughts drifted back to my older son, Tim, as he completed his homework on this mahogany desk. When Tim headed off to Harvard, his younger brother Nate claimed the desk for his own.

Wiping the desk, I reflected on how empty my home felt in the three weeks since Nate drove off in a van with friends for his freshman orientation at Georgetown. With both sons gone, the grounding role of mom shifted out from underneath me.

After 20 years of child rearing and caretaking, my nest was decidedly empty. Ignoring the dull aches at this loss, I had told a friend that if my kids were leaving the nest, so was I. I had planned to fly to London the next day for the first half of a sabbatical year, and then return to the U.S. in late December to spend time with the boys during Christmas break at my parents' house in Florida.

In January, I would pop into my office at Lesley College Graduate School for a few weeks to check on the progress of the International Studies Program I had initiated the previous year.

In late January, I expected to depart for Paris and head west until I circumnavigated the globe—arriving in San Francisco by late June. This ambitious itinerary sprang from the brain of Joseph Mestenhauser, an experienced international consultant brought to our fledgling program through a small grant I wrote. Upon examining my original travel plans, which focused on Europe, he proclaimed, "You can't run this program without some experience in the developing world. I'll draw up a better itinerary for you." And he did.

Cleaning my son's desktop was my final task to get the house ready for its new tenants, but I wasn't ready to go. I loved our house. The boys and I moved here after my marriage broke up six years previously. We learned to remake our family on the three floors of this small, yellow Victorian. After we settled in, I slowly refurbished the house from top to bottom, bringing it back to life, room by room, with paint and flowered wallpaper. The boys and I gradually came to enjoy our daily lives in the embrace of this warm and welcoming home.

I continued polishing the desktop in a last effort to leave this jewel of a place in tip-top condition. How could I possibly say good-bye to this home, to my kids, to my daily world? What in heaven's name had prompted me to undertake this crazy adventure?

Stumbling Blocks

A year earlier, I had hugged myself with excitement in anticipation of a sabbatical. After trips to Ireland and London, I longed for extended time abroad, which matched my current work in International Studies. However, finances were a challenge with two kids in college. I owned my house, so I could rent it to cover the mortgage and taxes. While I had the good fortune to receive a sabbatical year, I needed to augment my half-year salary, so I applied for the Mary Elvira Stevens Traveling Fellowship from Wellesley College.

When I read about it in the Wellesley College alumnae magazine, two weeks before an application date of December 1st, I dropped the magazine and picked up a pen—working furiously on my application. The following March, I drove to Wellesley College for an interview as one of four finalists. While my meeting went well, I grew disheartened when I encountered the excellence of the other contenders. Without the fellowship funding, my sabbatical plans would be shipwrecked. This realization sent me reeling.

A week later the phone rang; I picked up and heard the Chairwoman of the Stevens Committee say, "Hello Bonnie". Everything around me became still. I stared at the orange and yellow flowered wallpaper my friend Debby and I had installed in my kitchen.

"Congratulations!" she exclaimed. "I'm calling to say you won the fellowship."

"I won! I won!" I screamed when I hung up the phone, in sufficient volume to bring my son, Nate, who had commandeered his brother's space on the third floor, running down two flights of stairs. He picked me up and whirled me around three times, "You did it, Mum. You did it!"

I had done it. In hindsight, I believe the universe conspired to send me on this incredible midlife voyage. Think about it. In order to set out: my kids had to be in college; my parents had to be in good health; I had to be able to rent my house; I had to receive a grant to bring a consultant to the program I headed; he had to recommend round-the-globe travel; I had to be eligible for and granted a year's sabbatical; and finally I had to win a Cinderella-like fellowship to support it. As a good friend and colleague observed, "You've been gifted with a narrow window in your life right now that you can fly right through."

The Midlife Passage

I did not know it then, but I was caught up in a powerful transition. Phrases and sentences in my application for the Stevens Fellowship point towards a woman entering the midlife passage: "At midlife I stand poised at the proverbial turning point with a Janus-like view of past and future. For more than a decade I have been simultaneously cultivating the fields of family, graduate study, and profession. And now a confluence of events in my life and a quiet interior voice, to which I occasionally pay heed, are commanding me to stop and rest."

With a busy career, I mistakenly assumed my emptying nest an insignificant matter. I actually believed it was a joke when I told my friends, "If my kids are leaving the nest, so am I!" I dismissed the feelings of sadness that occasionally washed over me as I envisioned living alone in a three-story house.

An emptying nest is a classic example of a trigger that wakes you up at midlife, reminds you the old ways will not work any more, and then sets you on a quest to find more in yourself and in your life.

In later years when I became Dean of Continuing Education at Wellesley College, I often heard the return-to-college women I advised mention similar triggers.

- "I saw my daughter heading off for college and I asked myself, why can't I go, too?"
- "Now that my kids are in school all day, I have time to focus more on what I want to do!"

- "My real estate business is highly successful, but I felt seriously bored until one day, last summer, a friend told me she was going back to school."

What about you? Perhaps some trigger has propelled you into the midlife passage, where you find your usual rules for living are no longer valid. You may feel set adrift and lost, and stymied as to how to develop a new game plan.

The Magic Ingredient for Your Midlife Odyssey

The first step you can take and the best way to support yourself as a midlife traveler is to construct a soothing self-care regime. The book you hold in your hands will help you do just that. I wish I'd been able to tuck *Midlife Magic* in my suitcase during my year of sabbatical travel. It would have insured a far easier journey mentally, emotionally, and physically.

That transformative voyage generated the ideas for this book and my professional experience in the years that followed cemented their value. During my work as a dean for return-to-college women and later as a life coach for women at the mid-life crossroads, I have learned that self care is a critical ingredient for a successful midlife transition. Without it, the journey is far more challenging.

Installing a self-care regimen provides you with renewed energy and reduces your stress level. Your healthier body and attitude give you a greater sense of well being and confidence. Finally, the greater calm it produces allows you to face the challenges of the midlife metamorphosis with a fresh perspective and a grin that can't be contained.

So What Is Self Care

Anne Yeomans, a colleague and friend, defined self care as caring for yourself with wisdom and kindness. Thomas Leonard, a founding father of life coaching, described what he called "extreme self care" as "going to great lengths to show affection and concern for oneself" as opposed to "just enough care," which he indicated was "taking just enough action to prevent damage or harm." This "extreme self care," or what one of my clients called "radical self care" is the kind I prescribe in this book—the type that requires you to pay more attention to your own well being than ever before and step up to a new level of attending to your needs.

In this book you will discover seven skills to build your self-care system—one for each day of the week.

DAY 1: Self Compassion

DAY 2: Happy Body

DAY 3: Supportive Connections

DAY 4: Optimal Organization

DAY 5: Nurturing Environment

DAY 6: Time on Your Terms

DAY 7: Completion/Celebration

How to Use This Book

As you read through *Midlife Magic,* you will be able to adopt these seven self-care skills one day at a time. When you begin each day, you will find me in a different place on my sabbatical trip running into a need for that particular skill whether I realize it or not. You will explore each unique skill and learn how to develop it in your own life while encountering some real examples of how other women use this skill in their lives. And you'll find several suggested actions for engaging this skill, and choose one action to implement that very day.

For example, on DAY 1 you will read about my brush with *Self Compassion* in London, England. You will learn how to gain this particular skill and the ways other women practice it. And you will employ it yourself by selecting one *Self Compassion* action to follow right away.

On DAY 2 you will find me in Richmond, England, uncovering my need for a *Happy Body*, and again dive into more information about acquiring this skill and how other women on a midlife quest adopt it. You can practice it right away yourself by engaging a *Happy Body* action. As you continue, by the end of the week you will have installed a transforming program of "radical self care" for yourself. With this magic ingredient for supporting your midlife transformation, you will be a more resilient traveler, making your journey easier and more enjoyable.

If you like, you can find a friend to join you for a week of implementing this new self-care regime. You will be able to hold each other accountable and support one another along the way.

By practicing these seven self-care skills on a regular basis, you will reduce your daily stress and increase your energy, so you can give your inner world the attention the midlife passage requires. If you've been tending to loved ones for years, you will find this program of extreme self care a wonderful balance to your habit of automatically caring for others. You may even be surprised to find yourself smiling or laughing more often.

Once your basic self-care regime is established, if you want to advance a particular skill like *Optimal Organization*, you can return to this book—days, months, or even years later—

and select a second *Optimal Organization* action to adopt. With every return visit, you will take better and better care of yourself—after all, you are the person traveling through this transformative time. This most courageous woman needs your care and protection. My hope is *Midlife Magic* will increase your resiliency as you travel through these challenging and rewarding middle years of change and reinvention.

Let's begin!

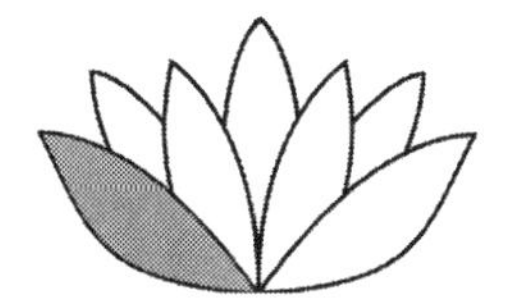

DAY 1: Self Compassion

London, England – September 1980

Squeaking luggage wheels jangled my nerves as I dragged my bags across cobblestone streets toward the International Students House (ISH) in northern London. Despite my lack of sleep on the plane to Heathrow, I moved at a quickened pace to reach my new abode.

Alone in an overwhelming metropolis, my thoughts traveled to my kids and my friends going about their daily routines across the ocean. Aching to get to ISH, I hurried along, wanting to settle into a place I could call home—if only for a week or so.

This residence for international students proved to be a perfect landing spot and quickly became a comfortable domicile. A pub in the basement and a tearoom on the second floor made meeting people easy—plus Friday nights brought "dance-time" featuring recorded music by this hot, new band called *The Police.*

While I longed to remain at ISH, my agreement required departure within a few weeks because I lacked the requisite enrollment in a formal educational program. After a week or so, a growing disquietude reminded me of this need for more permanent quarters

As I sat comfortably in the tearoom one day pondering this concern, I slumped further down in my chair when I pictured myself touring the streets of London knocking on doors of buildings with room-for-rent signs. I straightened up quickly when I remembered Jack.

A few days before leaving home, I met with an MD who specialized in supplements. I wanted my immune system to be as strong as possible because I would be traveling through the developing world in future months. Upon hearing I was departing for London in three days, he asked, "Do you have housing?"

"No."

He then mentioned a good friend of his, Jack, who owned a number of bedsits for international students and suggested Jack might well have one available. He handed me a slip of paper with Jack's phone number.

With this memory, I jumped out of my chair, located the slip of paper in my dorm room and headed for one of those iconic, red, British phone booths to call Jack. After listening to my introductory chatter, he asked if I would be willing to meet him at the East End docks at noon—evidently his stolen boat had just been returned from Brazil.

"Sure," I replied, counting on someone at ISH to direct me there. Sadly, I inherited my mother's lost-in-space gene, rather than my Dad's stellar orienting talents.

That afternoon found me on Jack's boat, sipping wine and munching sandwiches with a collection of his friends on a lazy, sunny fall day. My New England sensibilities were tuned to crisp weather and trees ablaze in autumn, but I delighted in this replacement of muted colors and soft warmth—a happy distraction from my ongoing trepidation about locating a place to live.

Later that day, Jack drove me to his mother's flat both to meet her and discuss housing possibilities. En route, my response to his first question about whether or not I wanted central heating came quickly, "definitely central heating".

Following a brief conservation with his mother, Jack led me upstairs to view his flat, where someone had recently moved out of the extra bedroom. He suggested I might move into it, noting he would be gone most of the time on business, so I would usually have the whole flat to myself for ridiculously low rent.

This fortuitous offer arose from an aspect of English real estate law according to Jack. He owned the entire building—a gorgeous edifice in Holland Park. According to the law, if he rented space to anyone undesirable, he had no legal ability to evict that person, because they became "sitting tenants". Since I would be departing in three months, I was an ideal occupant.

I could hardly believe this good fortune. My image of wandering through London endlessly in search of housing within my narrow price range evaporated like water in the desert. It didn't take me long to say yes to Jack's offer.

True to his word, he spent most of his time abroad, so I had this charming flat all to myself with its kitchenette featuring two burners and an electric tea kettle, plus my bedroom and a sitting room—both of which overlooked a small, enchanting garden park. Enclosed by a tall, wrought-iron fence and gate to which I had a key, I later came to think of it as "The Secret Garden"—my favorite book of childhood.

I never came to know Jack well, but his mother, Connie, and I became fast friends. She was a true character. At 72, she had been married three times—first to a colonel in the British army, whom she followed to Arabia where they became well acquainted with the local sheik (pronounced shake). I cannot remember what she told me about her second husband, but she moved to Australia when she married her third, who was a sheep farmer. Connie knew everything, and I mean absolutely everything, about sheep farming.

She had a wicked sense of humor that made my stomach hurt with laughter and a gift for playing Brahms' concertos on the piano that made me weep. A baby grand with an extraordinary sound swallowed up half of her sitting room. Delius, the renowned British composer, learned to play on this very instrument and the famous British pianist Myra Hess gave concerts on it.

After dinner most nights of the week, Connie played classical pieces by Mozart, Bach, Beethoven, and Brahms, while Danny, a young woman who just graduated from the Royal College of Music, Tim, and I gathered around to listen. Tim, a young man in his twenties, worked for the BBC as a graphic designer and knew more about art than anyone I'd ever met. Danny usually sang a song or two in her gorgeous operatic voice, and we always ended the evening belting out Noel Coward songs together, while Connie continued to play.

Far away from home, truly on my own for the first time in my life and more frightened than I realized, Connie provided the support I needed. I remember her once saying to me, "You want a family dear; it sticks out a mile."

Looking back, I see the utter truth of her statement. My unconscious need for family led me to find one with the instincts of a homing pigeon. Connie and her coterie of young friends served as my unofficial host family in this foreign land.

Tim and I visited museums regularly. He taught me to look for the use of black in Whistler's paintings and introduced me to the lesser-known charms of smaller venues like Lord Leighton House. Connie escorted me to view the wonders of Hamden Court. We traveled on the underground because her MINI Cooper had broken down on the I-96 while she and her current Australian boyfriend Maurice returned from an earlier visit to Hamden Court.

With her love for music, Connie and I soaked up concerts of her selection at the Royal Albert Hall. One evening, as we enjoyed a dish of ice cream during intermission, Connie spooned up every possible bit of this creamy confection, then lifted her bowl to lick it clean all the while grinning like a Cheshire Cat. I roared at her irreverence.

Later that fall, when I needed minor surgery, Connie accompanied me to Guy's Hospital with a promise to pick me up the next day after my discharge. Her care was so natural that only the night before the surgery did I realize it might be a good idea to let someone at home know I was going under the knife. Not wanting to worry my kids, I made a quick phone call to my parents.

True to her word, Connie fetched me the next day. Somehow, her MINI Cooper had reappeared—repaired and ready to go. She cooked lamb chops and spinach for supper to "build up your strength, dear."

No matter how many years I had to prepare for an emptying nest, I wasn't ready to live without my family. While compassion for others came early and perhaps too easily for me, I hadn't developed the skill of self compassion, which would have given me more strength to face the challenges of this transitional period. Connie provided all the compassion and family I required in this bridge time before my future adventure into strange lands alone.

Our friendship was mutual. I evidently gave Connie something, too—good company and a companion who appreciated her and relished her wit. When I left, she asked me to send her someone else please, "preferably like yourself, dear, with a bit of a giggle."

HOW TO DEVELOP SELF COMPASSION

Connie's daily presence on the first leg of my journey offered the lifesaving raft I needed. Without her kindness and compassion I would have drowned before embarking on my travels into more unfamiliar worlds. I had not yet developed the self compassion I needed for the voyage ahead.

The midlife journey can challenge your very soul—it did mine. A well-developed skill of self compassion will help you meet the demands of this transitional time—an ability so critical it holds the primary spot of Day 1.

Definition of Self Compassion

This essential for building resilience can be defined as viewing and treating yourself with the same kindness and affection that Connie gave me. People thrive in this kind of environment and you will, too, just the way I did.

If you are like many women, you have far more compassion for your family and friends than you do for yourself. You may not be aware of your own needs, or truly accept yourself for who you are. With a regard for others, you may also find it difficult to say NO in your day-to-day interactions. Let's examine these three areas to see where you can make some changes and strengthen your self-compassion muscles.

Become More Self Aware

The starting point for developing the skill of self compassion is self awareness—i.e. being present to the world within you and the world around you. You can accomplish this feat by bringing attention to your physical, mental, and emotional worlds.

Become more aware of your body. Why not tune into your body and its senses right now? Are you sitting down? Sense the weight of your body on the chair or couch. Are your legs crossed? If so, feel the pressure where one overlaps the other. Now take a minute and focus on your breathing. Notice your inhale and exhale for three counts. See how easy bringing your awareness to your body can be.

Attention to your other senses can also be simple. Look around you for a minute. What do you see? Pause for a moment, what do you hear? Can you locate any smells?

And if you grab that cup of coffee or tea, is it really hot? And how does it taste? Have you noticed how calming these mini activities are? Do you realize you have not been traveling in the land of your mind while doing them?

Become aware of your thoughts. The realm of the mind is trickier to navigate, because it takes you out of the present moment and plops you into the past, or the future. There are two different types of thoughts to consider in developing your awareness of the mind's activities. The first kind is when you consciously focus on an issue like trying to solve a problem. These thoughts are easy to notice. The second kind arises unbidden from your unconscious and reflects patterns learned in childhood as a way of grappling with the world around you. This not-so-easily-observed conditioned thought pattern repeats itself daily and generates your emotions automatically.

Meditation offers one way to follow the movements of the mind. If you sit in a relaxed position for even five minutes with a focus on your breathing you will probably find yourself distracted with thoughts—one after the other. Meditation instructors suggest you allow these thoughts to freely float away and bring your focus back to your breathing. Heading for the land of the body—when your thoughts take those negative repetitive rides like a gerbil on a wheel—can be wonderfully disruptive. You simply cannot bring your attention to your body and your mind simultaneously.

Become more aware of your emotions. Your emotions are easier to spot. Feelings like joy and anger make themselves known readily. Picture yourself driving down the highway; suddenly a car cuts in front of you with no warning causing you to brake quickly. You may naturally shake your head, or cuss out the "thoughtless" driver. Can you become aware of that naturally induced anger, observe it, and let it go to the point where you can truly say, "welcome to my lane" without rancor? This process is clearly challenging, but worth your effort—far better than returning to this event in your mind—giving rise to your anger, again and again just thinking about it. Truth be told, you have no control over that "thoughtless" driver.

Accept Your Self

Self acceptance lies at the heart of self compassion. A welcoming stance to both the darker and brighter sides of your psyche brings surprising rewards. If you're like many midlife women, more often than not, you automatically put on *mean girl* glasses when it comes to observing yourself—which doesn't make for a happy self, or a happy life. Imagine for a minute that you couldn't easily let go of your anger at that crazy driver who cut in front of you, and you continued to replay the event and your frustration in your mind. Upon observing this replay, would you be gentle with yourself, or might you berate yourself a little for being unable to release that emotion?

How do you find *kind girl* glasses for observing yourself? One way to locate them is to remember the ones you don when propping up a friend or encouraging a child. The trick here is to continue wearing these *kind girl* specs when you turn your attention back to yourself—especially when you've messed up. It's a bit tempting and perhaps even habitual, to automatically grab the familiar *mean girl* shades to examine yourself when you make a mistake.

The first step to locating your *kind girl* specs is to become aware of when you're wearing the *mean girl* ones. When one of my coaching clients, Eliza, first began to track her daily self talk, she was astonished and then mortified at how often *mean girl* arrived. After just one day, she discovered that *kind girl* hadn't poked her head around the corner even once!

On the morning of her tracking day, she made a double batch of banana bread for her family, but forgot to double the amount of flour. When she noticed the soupy consistency of the batter, her *mean girl* arrived with the classic remark, "What a stupid mistake!"

When Eliza went to add the missing flour, *mean girl's* remark upset her so much, she dropped the measuring cup on the floor. Since it was stainless, the cup didn't break, but her *mean girl* couldn't resist adding, "Now look what you've done!"

In talking with me later about her experience of tracking *mean girl* and *kind girl*, Eliza acknowledged that *kind girl* never made her presence known. When I asked what *kind girl* might have said, Eliza replied, "Aren't you thoughtful to be making a treat for your family, or aren't you clever to be making two loaves so you can freeze one!"

When I pressed further about how *kind girl* might respond to the forgotten flour or the dropped measuring cup, Eliza laughed. "I might say something like, 'We all make mistakes, and as mistakes go this one is pretty minor and easily fixed.' "

"What about a big mistake, that's not so easily fixed?"

"Hmm…mm, maybe something like, 'I guess I'm human after all and I can work to do better in the future. I accept my frailty. And I can apologize if needed.' "

Eliza located her *kind girl* specs. And you can too. With conscious awareness you can discover how much *mean girl* dominates and how to bring *kind girl* out of hiding. Let her perspective take over as you gradually become more gentle with yourself. You can stop beating yourself up with daily remarks like, "How could I have been so stupid?" Or, "I'm such a loser." (Hair shirts went out with the Middle Ages.) Or even trickier—not judge yourself for holding onto your thoughts and emotions like the frustration you might feel when a car cuts you off unannounced. This kind of personal-observation growth work takes practice and time.

Carl Jung, the famous Swiss psychiatrist, referred to the midlife transition as a shift from the morning to the afternoon of life. For him, embracing the shadow (those elements of the psyche that have been repressed, denied, and/or rejected) is the key to making that shift successfully. Your *mean girl* lives in that shadow. To bring her into consciousness, you must travel through the land of the shadow. When you first come upon her, you may simply run away, cringe a bit, or judge her harshly—donning your *mean girl* glasses again!

Simply accept this gal as part how you have tried to protect yourself in the past. Be gentle with her; don your *kind girl* glasses. Remember your own goodness and sink into the soft folds of your own compassion.

Learn to Say NO

Taking care of yourself also means saying NO to the requests from family, friends, and acquaintances when that's what you want to do. The habits of a lifetime may impel you to respond to such appeals with an automatic YES. Learning to assess the implications of such invitations and finding ways to say NO requires attention and time as one of my clients discovered.

Valerie called on my services because she felt totally overwhelmed. Her life seemed to be unraveling with her stress level increasing every day. She craved more balance in her life. After our initial self-discovery sessions, we compiled a list of all the projects she had undertaken—ultimately constructing an Excel spreadsheet with a lineup of these projects. She then scheduled timing and to-dos for each project.

The spreadsheet made it easy to see why Valerie felt swamped. We examined each project, one by one, as she explained how and why she had undertaken it. While each one appeared exciting at the time and always benefited others, each one now carried an oppressively long list of to-dos. In hindsight, when Valerie reviewed them through the lens of her own desires and the time required to complete each project, some proved far more compelling and interesting than others.

Valerie gradually scoped out and scheduled what was needed to bring her current commitments to completion. Together we developed criteria for future projects Valerie might enjoy, and determined some "stay-away" signs for those that might not prove deeply satisfying even if helpful to others. Valerie began to see the possibility and value of saying NO.

Learning to assess future possibilities and finding ways to say NO is a process that will not happen quickly.

You can start small the way Valerie did. First she decided before she said YES to any appeal, she would take 24 hours to determine how it might benefit her in addition to others. Then she estimated the costs (especially the time) required to honor the request. This new plan required her to say NO when she decided there was less benefit to her than other possible commitments.

For Valerie—and any woman who has not yet developed the skill of self compassion—considering yourself when making a decision is a new behavior. If you already take at least 24 hours before you respond to any request, you are on your way to developing this important skill. If you do not, adopting this rule is a great way to begin. You're not only comporting yourself differently, but also changing the habits of a lifetime. Sometimes it's helpful to remember that a NO can be as good as YES.

The good news about focusing your attention on this DAY 1 attribute is that a research review by Neff and Dahm reveals that developing self-compassion leads to higher levels of optimism, well-being, and happiness. Now who doesn't want some of that?

TAKE ACTION

Are you ready to develop this DAY 1 skill of *Self Compassion*? It's simple. Select one action to implement today from the 10 possible steps listed below. I recommend you choose the easiest one, or the one that screams, "Pick me!"

1. Every time you get up out of a chair, practice bringing awareness to your body. Sounds simple, doesn't it?

2. When you stand at the sink in your kitchen, instead of thinking about what you have to do next, bring your attention to your body as it moves to wash the lettuce, load the dishwasher, wash your hands, or whatever you are there to do.

3. Try out this brief mindfulness meditation—the 5-4-3-2-1 exercise. Start with a deep breath in and out. Simply count to four as you breathe in and five as you breathe out. Then, look around the room and name five things you can see. Next, move your focus into your body and name four things you can feel. Then, bring your attention to your hearing and name three things you can hear. Next, focus on what you can smell and name two things you can smell—or imagine two things you like to smell. Finally, name one thing you can taste, or like to taste. Remember to relax your breath, and if a judgment or an unwanted thought comes into your mind, simply observe it and let it go. This is a great exercise to use whenever your mind hops on the worry wheel.

4. When your phone rings today, before you answer it quickly out of habit, take a deep breath or two, center yourself, then connect and say hello. This practice will serve you well in the future and is super easy to implement.

5. Spend a day tracking your self talk to observe when *mean girl* and *kind girl* arrive. Remember to be gentle when *mean girl* arrives! This action step is more challenging to implement, but you may be surprised at the benefits it can bring.

6. Schedule a specific time today for a mindfulness break—no emails, no texts, and no screens—continue this practice every day.

7. Try this simple exercise. Focus on one arm. Simply move it up, be aware, pause, then let it back down. Do the same with the other arm. Why not start right now? Repeat it a few times throughout the day.

8. The next time a request comes your way from anyone—friend, family, or colleague, be sure to take 24 hours to give your response. Consider whether you truly have the desire and energy to accomplish it. One easy way to say NO, is to say YES to another aspect of the task. For example, if you do not wish to make a pie for the school bake sale, you could offer to help out on the day of the sale. Or you could say, "I'm not going to be able to bake this fall, but I'll plan to work for the spring book sale."

9. Spend a morning or afternoon naming ways you appreciate your actions. Be sure to take this to the extreme. Some examples follow. "How wonderful of me to wake up and start the day, instead of relaxing in bed for another half hour." "What a marvelous mom I am to cook breakfast for the kids!" "How great of me to head for work to help support myself (and my family)." While you may feel silly applauding yourself for what seems routine, it will make you conscious of how you can appreciate all that you do in a day. Since we tend to focus more on negative thoughts, emphasizing the positive will help develop your

self compassion. We need lots of positive thoughts to balance each negative one.

10. Your choice! You create an action that will further develop your self compassion.

Which action did you choose to implement?

____

Now TAKE ACTION!

Later you can treat yourself to a good night's sleep, and look forward to adding another self-care skill to your repertoire tomorrow.

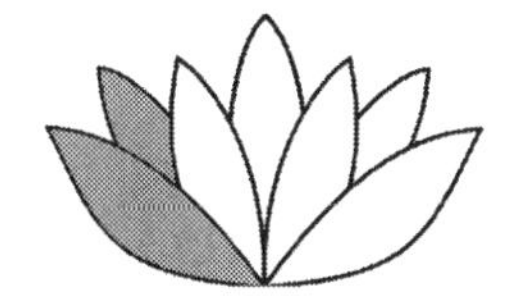

DAY 2: Happy Body

Richmond, England – November 1981

The pastoral English landscape rolled by my window on a train out of central London, while my thoughts turned to what lay ahead at Southlands College. A few weeks ago Professor Tuku Mukherjee, the head of its Dip Ed (Diploma of Education) program in Multicultural Education, asked me to come for a visit when we met at a conference in Brighton. Since he ran the only program of its kind in England, I was eager to learn from him. It also happened to be my birthday, so I welcomed a bit of adventure to celebrate the day.

With Tuku's clear directions, I easily found my way from the train station to his office. Checking my watch before entering his brightly lit domain, I stood a little straighter when I realized I was right on time. It was precisely 9:30 am. One of the more challenging aspects of my travel in England was arriving punctually for professional appointments—especially since I traveled via public transportation to places unknown. Happily, British rail, the oldest rail system in the world, proved to be incredibly reliable.

When I entered Tuku's office, he rose from his chair and walked toward me, extending a hand in welcome. Gesturing to a coffee pot sitting under a bank of windows, he offered to pour me a cup. I gratefully accepted. We sat down and chatted a while about his newly created multicultural education program open to teachers with more than five years of experience. He ended our conversation by suggesting we join the students in his class, where I might speak a bit about education in America. Despite this unexpected invitation to talk about the American educational system, I was eager to meet his students.

We found them down the hall and around the corner in a large room furnished only with a mammoth square table with an empty center constructed out of those ubiquitous 30"/90" function tables. Surrounding the table on four sides were 16 students, patiently seated in white, plastic, Danish modern chairs with chrome legs.

Tuku introduced the students one by one as I learned they came from countries all over the world including Cyprus, Barbados, India, and Pakistan. Their brown and black faces affirmed these origins with one exception—the only woman in the program, who hailed from Manchester, England. Her pale, freckled face and springy, red curls provided remarkable contrast to the dark hair and complexions of the men around the table.

I embarked on a brief overview of the American educational system including our community colleges, which I knew foreign visitors to the US often found intriguing. Then the students peppered me with questions.

This Q & A period led to lively discussions on many topics until I felt a sudden warmth between my legs. I knew at once what caused it. Recently, excessive bleeding during my periods due to fibroids led me to consult a Harley Street physician, so I knew the warmth I felt was menstrual blood.

I turned to Tuku, who was seated at the head of the table, and said as quietly as I could with some urgency, "I need to use the ladies washroom."

He stood up promptly. I followed him rapidly out of the room, back down the hall, and around a corner where he pointed to a door marked "WC".

"Do join us when you can," he said turning to leave.

I zipped into the washroom, found the nearest stall and discovered I had bled through layers of feminine protection, my underwear, and onto my skirt. Luckily, it was black wool so the blood barely showed. I cleaned up as best I could, replacing the layers of protective items. Thanks to an empty washroom, I could wash out my nylon underpants in the sink and dry them with the pressurized-air hand dryer, which fortunately worked well. I blotted my skirt with some available tissues and tucked a few extra tissues into my pocketbook.

Finally, I deemed myself presentable enough to return to the classroom, but my body seemed frozen in place—unable to move. What to do? I couldn't remain in the bathroom all day, and departing without saying goodbye to Tuku seemed incredibly rude. I reluctantly opened the door into the hall and proceeded back to join the others.

Before entering the classroom, I paused in the doorway to garner a bit of strength. Eying my empty chair, I spotted a small pool of blood underneath it. Oh no! Surreptitiously taking a tissue out of my pocketbook, I walked over to the chair, crouched down to wipe up the blood, and tucked the used tissue in the outside pocket of my bag. When I stood up and pulled out the chair to sit down, a gleaming red circle on the white seat came into view. I grabbed another tissue, disposed of the blood in similar fashion, and sat down.

Momentarily mortified, I conjured up the menstrual taboos the men's cultures or religions might harbor. "Unclean" or "embarrassing" would probably be on the list. "Talking about women's menses" would certainly be verboten. I had managed a public demonstration of menstruation, which lived in a realm "beyond taboo"—not to mention that "bloody" was an English swear word. Again, as no other option came to mind, I entered the discussion as though nothing had happened.

When the class ended, Tuku escorted me back to his office. Expecting him to be relieved by my departure, an incredulous look passed over my face when he invited me to join him for lunch followed by forays into the multiethnic communities to see their efforts in action.

I replied with a startled, "I'd love to!"

That afternoon provided a fascinating glimpse into other worlds—a perfect precursor to the journey that lay ahead of me. We lunched at a local Indian restaurant. In those days, Indian restaurants were rare in the States, but they were abundant in parts of London and usually very good. I found this one to be no exception as I enjoyed the scent and taste of spicy dal soup and filled up on deliciously flavored Tandoori chicken.

After lunch Tuku took me to meet a friend he had in this multicultural community. We found our way to a third floor attic apartment where a tan, wrinkled, white-haired Tibetan woman brewed Chai tea for us. Sipping the warm, spicy, black tea sweetened with milk and honey took the edge off a very cold November day and provided welcome comfort after a challenging morning. Her daughter joined us later, and, over sips of tea, related an inspiring story of how she had developed a community preschool, which was now in full swing.

Later, we walked to the local Boys Club while Tuku described the racial tensions between the West Indian and Indian teenagers in the town. Their Boys Club project aimed to find ways of bringing the two groups together through sports, card games (including bridge), and other activities after school.

On the train ride back to London, I mused on the happenings of the day. Despite my feelings of profound helplessness and embarrassment, my English birthday turned out to be "bloody" marvelous! I never did find out if any of the students or Tuku noticed the blood. While I would meet with Tuku again, he never mentioned it and I never asked.

I also realized the hormone therapy my Harley Street physician proscribed wasn't working, so I would need a D&C—the next step in the treatment plan she outlined.

My eyes softened when I thought about this doctor. Her warm demeanor and light-filled office put me immediately at ease on my first visit there. The sight of a folded mohair throw in a light blue and green tartan placed at the end of the examining table, in lieu of stirrups and a strip of paper, relaxed me even further.

After taking a medical history and listening to a description of my recent life, she leaned forward to say, "You strike me as a can-do kind of gal who has faced continual stress in recent years. I find when stress is ongoing, men get ulcers and women bleed."

Her words rang true. My life was way out of balance. At some level, I knew this truth before embarking on my trip when I wrote that sentence in my fellowship application, "A confluence of events and a quiet interior voice, to which I occasionally pay heed, are commanding me to stop and rest."

I did not have a happy body at the time. It took me many more years to find it. Why wait? You can have a happy body today!

HOW TO DEVELOP A HAPPY BODY

Please notice I said, "You can have a happy body." I did not say, "You can be happy about your body." The current American culture with its never-ending images and text reminding women and girls they are not thin enough, tall enough, or sufficiently "bootylicious" or "boobalicious," make that goal beyond the scope of this book. But again, you can have a happy body—your self-care skill for DAY 2.

Developing this skill will put you in shape to meet the natural physical, emotional, and mental stresses that midlife often brings.

A Simple Exercise

I invite you to imagine for a moment that you and your body are consulting a therapist. After speaking with you for a while, the therapist turns to your body and asks, "How has (fill in your name here) been treating you of late?"

If the answer is something like "Beautifully! She attends to my needs the way a new mom cares for her baby. I couldn't ask for more," then please skim the rest of the chapter and focus your attention for today on more urgent matters. You already have a happy body. If, on the other hand, your body suggests you've been ignoring it of late, or even abusing it, now's the time to put your body on the happiness track. An easy injunction for improving your physical well being is, "Move well; eat well; rest well."

It sounds simple, but acting on this advice may seem daunting if you're living in a land of uncertainty and overwhelmed like many women at midlife. For this reason, we will move forward only one step at a time. Remember after you finish reading this how-to section of Day 2, you choose just one step to implement in the Take Action section.

You will undoubtedly find the following suggestions familiar, as they are derived from common knowledge, along with my clients' experience, and my own. They provide a template for putting together a personal *Happy Body* plan that works for you and your lifestyle. As always, be sure to consult with an appropriate health care professional before you undertake any new physical activities.

Move Well

Like me, perhaps your empty nest has left you floundering. Or perhaps, you're more like Selena, one of my clients who was eager to go back to work now that both her kids were in elementary school. Before her two boys arrived, Selena made a living as a highly successful marketing executive in California, but marriage and children brought her back to the East Coast as a stay-at-home mom. When the workplace called again, she wanted to use her marketing background in a different way.

She didn't want to travel the way she used to, because she valued being home for her kids and also hoped to find a workplace with an easy commute. In addition, she preferred to ease slowly back into the job market with a part-time position. Finally, she didn't want to work out of her home, because she longed for some adult company every day.

When I first work with clients, we set up areas of focus for our coaching time together. What brought Selena to coaching was her strong wish to reenter the job market, so that desire sat at the top of our focus list. She also wanted to start running again, so an exercise program became number two.

While finding her ideal job naturally took a bit of time, Selena began running the first day after our coaching session, after her boys hopped on the school bus. One of the benefits of this *Happy Body* skill is that you can start developing it right away. During the next few weeks at the beginning of each coaching call, Selena thrilled to tell me she had gone running on a local bike path—three, or sometimes four times a week. She also noticed how this exercise gave her energy for all the informational interviews she initiated to find her way back into the job market.

One of the more powerful aspects of life coaching is its structure of weekly accountability. Clients often tell me they completed their promised action of the week the day before our call, because they knew they were going to be speaking with me. You too can take advantage of this powerful motivating mechanism.

Why not set up an accountability partner for whatever exercise goals you want to accomplish? Maybe you can find a jogging buddy, or a friend to head to the gym with you. Human nature being what it is, if you agree to meet a friend to go running, or join you at the gym, you're more likely to show up. Perhaps you'd like to meet a friend at the gym for ballet or dance aerobics—or maybe find a bicycling buddy for weekly jaunts.

Most exercise programs focus on three areas of fitness: aerobic activity, muscle strength and endurance, and flexibility.

Find your aerobic activity. With her new running regime, Selena had her aerobic workout well in hand with an activity that just plain made her feel better.

Unlike Selena, Margaret never liked running. In fact a physical therapist once told her she shouldn't run on a regular basis, because she didn't have a runner's body. Margaret wasn't keen on the treadmill either. She never experienced the endorphin high that so many runners describe.

Nevertheless, Margaret recognized the need for some kind of ongoing cardiovascular activity, so she hopped on a treadmill at least three times a week. Instead of an endorphin high, her reward was the pleasure of reading a book with a compelling plot that she downloaded from the library onto her iPad. To build up her aerobic fitness, she regularly increased the incline on the treadmill, and occasionally even upped the walking speed.

With a little self examination, you can determine which cardio option works best for you. Maybe you're most like one of my clients, Kathy, who loves being in nature, so she takes long walks every day—rain or shine—to stay in shape and lower stress levels. Simply being in nature can also raise your happiness level.

Build your muscle strength and endurance. Building muscle strength and endurance, the second aspect of the fitness trinity, is often accomplished with weight training. Before you slide onto the seat of one of those weight machines at the gym, I suggest you spend time with a trained staff person to help you determine the appropriate settings and show you how to use them safely.

If gardening calls you regularly, you're engaging in a natural strength training activity. Selena decided that daily gardening would be her strength-building regime while she hunted for a job until the ground froze. In the winter, she planned to use her weights at home while she watched her favorite gardening programs on TV.

Develop your flexibility. After installing her treadmill-while-reading regime, Margaret debated a long time about whether to head for a yoga studio to develop her flexibility—the third prong of your fitness focus. She finally decided to accompany a friend to a local class to give it a try.

Stretching in the Hatha yoga poses enabled her to sense her body in a new way; for the first time she discovered the joy of moving.

Over time she became hooked on stretching; although she had to admit that her favorite pose came at the end of class where everyone lay down to relax on their mat in Shavasana, or corpse pose. She especially appreciated the facial massage the yoga instructor provided with a lavender-scented cream as a special bonus. She learned later this was not a usual part of most yoga classes.

Selena, on the other hand, tried yoga to increase her flexibility, but found it too slow for her temperament. Instead she amplified her regime of stretching before her run each day and supplemented it with other stretching exercises.

Eat Well

What kind of diet makes your body happy? By diet, I'm using the first two definitions from the Merriam-Webster Unabridged Dictionary:

> a: food and drink regularly provided or consumed
> b: habitual nourishment

Does your body do the happy dance about the food and drink you habitually consume? If not, time for some change.

Eliminate the negative. One of the simplest ways to improve your diet is to cut out any food or drink you know disappoints your body. Margaret started with potato chips. Every day at work she headed for the cafeteria where she ordered the sandwich of the day, which always arrived on her plate with a bag of chips. She decided to eliminate the chips on Monday through Thursday and enjoy their crunch on Fridays. After hanging out with other women in her yoga class for a few weeks, she also eliminated her favorite lunchtime Coke and substituted an unsweetened iced tea with lemon instead. With these two simple changes, she improved the daily mood of her body and—to her surprise—lost four pounds.

Lulu knew her body lumbered under the extra weight she carried around and wanted to lose it, but knew her diets of the past only yo-yoed her back to her current weight and then some. Sitting beside Margaret every day, she decided to join the potato chip elimination spree. While she and Margaret lost a few pounds this way, Lulu wanted to lose more and to establish a healthier lifetime eating regime.

She searched the Internet for the best ways to choose a weight loss diet and then consulted with her doctor, who recommended a health care provider specializing in weight loss. Lulu listened carefully as this woman explained the approach her doctor recommended. She was delighted to find she didn't have to cook special meals or count calories; all she needed to do was eat the packaged meals provided by the program. Her weight came off slowly, but consistently over time and she particularly liked the convenience of this approach.

If you want to lose weight, which is certainly a different goal than eating well (although the two often go together), be sure to work with a health care provider who can recommend a program, support your progress as you complete the program, and continue to work with you to help you maintain a healthy lifestyle to keep your body happy.

Accentuate the positive. For most folks, eating is a pleasure, so why not accentuate the positive here? When you chomp into that delicious Honeycrisp apple in the fall, be sure to relish the experience instead of distractedly reading a book or watching TV. As an acupuncturist I consulted that fall in London told me, "When you eat, eat; when you read, read."

Mean-spirited thoughts also take the edge off the sheer pleasure of consuming a delightful meal. Ever eaves-dropped on the conversation of ladies lunching together? Did you hear phrases like, "I know I shouldn't eat this," or "Goes right from my lips to my hips"? Margaret once asked me if I thought any small group of women could enjoy a meal together without some kind of comment about weight. I regretfully had to respond in the negative.

Your lunch mates' comments are not within your control, but your own thoughts can be examined and changed when necessary. Why not take a day to increase your awareness of your own thoughts whenever you eat? As you dive into a meal and find a judgmental thought bubbling up, simply pause for a moment and let it waft away. Instead, you can savor the tantalizing smell and colors of the meal in front of you, before you take a bite.

Remember, whatever eating regime you employ, this is your body and your life; the only comparisons you need to make are with yourself about your own progress.

> *The sooner you stop comparing yourself to other people, the more attention you get to put on yourself.*
>
> – Brooke Shields

Rest Well

Sleep. You undoubtedly know a restful night's sleep recharges your batteries for the next day, but do you know it also leads to a longer life and lots of other perks? WebMD lists 11 rewards of a restful night's sleep—all backed up by one research study or another:

- Better memory
- Live longer
- Curb inflammation
- Spur creativity
- Improve athletic ability
- Steer clear of depression
- Avoid accidents
- Improve your grades
- Sharpen attention
- Have a healthy weight
- Lower stress

If you already get a good night's sleep, great! If not, perhaps at least one of these 11 benefits will persuade you to seek the hours you need. If this kind of logic doesn't spur you to take action, perhaps some of the techniques outlined below will encourage you to reap the rewards of consistent, restorative sleep each night. If you have kids who don't seem to be getting their much-needed zzzs, these tips can help them too.

- Go to bed at the same time every night. Your body responds to consistent structure and if you hit the sack at the same time each night, you will find yourself feeling tired at just about that time.

- Stay off the screens two hours before bedtime. The backlighting of phones and tablets fool the brain into believing it's daytime, so the melatonin hormone that brings you sweet sleep isn't released as easily.

- Cover your bedroom windows with room darkening shades or curtains. If that's not possible, buy yourself a sleep mask to keep your bedroom dark—an invitation to the sleep-friendly melatonin.

- Keep all electronic equipment out of bedroom. No TV, no cell phone, no tablet. Think of how much those restful nights will mean to your daytime enjoyment.

- As you're heading into dreamland, count backwards from 500. This simple exercise engages the left side of your brain, so all those worrying thoughts that keep you awake at night float away.

- Sip some hot milk 15 minutes before bedtime to put the concerns of the day to rest.

- Head for bed earlier. Why not start with 15 minutes and build up to an hour? Experts suggest the deepest and most regenerative sleep occurs between 10 pm and 2 am.

Selena tried this last suggestion. She came to love her morning run that began when her sons stepped onto the school bus each day. After a couple of months, she had to stop this personally nurturing routine, because she landed that job she was seeking. And it was perfect—close to home, part time with no travel required! Plus it not only called on her past marketing experience, but also involved personally meaningful work. To continue her running that had come to mean so much, she decided to go to bed an hour earlier to wake up an hour earlier and finish her run before breakfast.

Sleep O sleep! O gentle sleep! Nature's soft nurse…

– William Shakespeare

Meditate. One of the best stress-busters of all time is meditation. We return to this ancient practice more fully on this DAY 2, because it provides physical—as well as mental—rest from the busy, busy days that characterize the lives of so many midlife women.

Think about it for a minute. Meditation is free, it's easy to learn, it doesn't require expensive equipment, and you can do it anywhere—a quick, easy route to inner peace and calm. What could be better?

If you already meditate, simply skip the next few paragraphs, head to the final section, and take action. On the other hand, if you'd like to take up this stress-busting practice, here are some tips to help you begin.

- Meditation is a process of quieting the mind, bringing you into the present moment. Thoughts, sensations, and feelings associated with the past or future are simply not there in that moment of time.

- To begin, you can simply sit in a relaxed position, and allow your eyes to close. Focus on your breathing—breath in; breath out. Or, if you like, you can repeat a calming word or phrase over and over.

- Or you may wish to listen to a recording for meditation; the Internet is full of them. Simply select an app that seems easiest and most appealing.

Margaret decided to add meditation to her midlife renewal practice after she found her Hatha yoga classes so rewarding. Her increased awareness of breathing from yoga class made it simple for her to sit in her favorite armchair and focus on her breath as it came into and out of her nostrils. Her meditation of only 10 minutes a day made it easy to stick to this regime and its calming influence.

- As you meditate, whenever intrusive thoughts naturally arrive, simply let them float away and bring your attention back to your breath, or calming word, or meditation music.

- Feel free to meditate in any location. If sitting on a cushion in lotus position doesn't sound delightful, why not use a comfortable chair just like Margaret? Or what about a quiet walk in nature? Or perhaps you'd feel fulfilled walking a labyrinth. Just remember to keep your focus on your breath, or on a word you repeat.

- Once you get the knack, you can meditate anywhere. What about easing into a meditative mode when stuck in a traffic jam? (Don't close your eyes, of course.) Or how about slipping into that peaceful world in the midst of a heated business meeting for half a minute?

- Remember to be aware of those tricky thoughts. Along with concerns about your to-do list, you may find more judgmental ideas popping up like, "Am I doing this right?" or, "I must be a bad meditator." Acknowledge the presence of these thoughts, then let them float away and return your focus to your breath.

- Watch external distractions. Maybe you hear the ping of an email or text and wonder if you should check it. That's just another thought—let it go—then head back to the feel and sound of your breath going in and out, or repeating your calming word.

Your meditation—however short or long—will initiate a practice of internal focus. Notice how with time you gain greater perspective on all the issues of your life. Your midlife journey will become easier because any successful transition is an inside job.

Your body is your first home. Treat it well.
– Anonymous

TAKE ACTION

Ready to get started? Simply select one of the action steps listed below to put *Happy Body* into practice. I recommend you start with the easiest exercise. The guiding mantra for successful change is to pick one step that works for you, implement it today, and continue to practice it every day moving forward. For example, if you choose Step #2. Meditate for five minutes, you would begin today and continue to meditate for five minutes every day moving forward.

On the other hand, if you pick a cumulative action step, you would add to it every day. For example if you choose Step #1, set up a plan for a cardio activity, you would devise the plan today and then implement the plan tomorrow and the days that follow.

Which one strikes your fancy?

1. Create a plan for taking up a cardio activity. Be sure to include specifically when, where and with whom you'll begin. Great way to start creating a *Happy Body*!

2. Meditate for five minutes. Surely you can spare five minutes.

3. Plop on that explorer's hat and scope out the yoga studios close to your work or home. Find a yoga class that is convenient and sign up to try one. Or find a yoga DVD or TV class so you can begin stretching at home.

4. Eliminate one item from your diet that makes your body unhappy. This step won't take any extra time.

5. Add one item to your diet that makes your body happy. Think about it—happy!

6. Go to bed 15 minutes earlier. Just 15 minutes, why not?

7. Develop your own action step and follow it. Might be the most effective route.

8. Purchase a sleep mask. Simply order one online—won't take long.

9. Stay off your phone, tablet, or computer two hours before bedtime. Try this experiment to see if you don't drop off into dreamland more easily.

10. Find an accountability partner for improving any *Healthy Body* practice. Why not choose this one—might be fun!

Which action did you choose?

I am willing to implement # __________

Now TAKE ACTION!

Later you can treat yourself to a good night's sleep, and look forward to adding another self-care skill to your repertoire tomorrow.

DAY 3: Supportive Connections

Maseru, Lesotho – March 1981

I heard a soft tapping on my hotel room door just before daybreak. Fully dressed, I stepped into the hall, closing the door quietly behind me. My former boss, Bill, and I crept down the stairs of the Molimo Nthuse Lodge, opened the front door softly, and headed toward the creek that ran behind the lodge. While my body lumbered forward with sleepy steps, a sense of charged anticipation found me wide-awake by the time we reached the riverbed. The magnetic possibility of hunting for gold there drew my positive response to Bill's invitation to everyone at the dinner table last night, "Who wants to go prospecting for gold in the morning?"

I was the only one who responded with a positive, "I'd love to!"

Any gold hunting needed to occur before breakfast if our crew followed the planned itinerary to reach the Saint James Mission School by nightfall. So the pre-dawn light found the two of us squatted with sieves in hand, scooping up sand and gravel from the riverbed, and inspecting it for any hint of a gold.

My excitement at this pursuit gave me an idea of what sent hundreds of thousands of men west to California in the gold rush of 1849. With an undergraduate major in geology, I had an affection for this dense, soft metal that never loses its luster, which is why we could find glints of it in the sandy gravel after thousands of years.

Bill's sense of adventure and fun was one of the qualities that made him the best boss I ever had—bar none. As Dean of the Graduate School at Lesley College, Bill's accomplishments were just short of miraculous. During his first five years in the role, student enrollment increased 42% every year. Yet, whenever I walked by his office, the door was open, his desk completely bare, and a smile filled his face as he beckoned me to come in for a chat. I never met a dean with such an open door policy, including myself in later years.

Bill's down-to-earth talent for growing people and programs revealed itself again in his role as an educational consultant to the Minister of Education for the country of Lesotho. Upon arrival, he observed file drawers full of reports from other consultants sent by U.S. AID. He took a different approach. In the fall of that year, he visited every single secondary school in this mountainous country with a simple question for every principal, "What three things would you like to change about your school?"

If he could fix any one of them right then, (i.e. replace a window), he did so. He then designed a national, three-day conference in the capital, Maseru, for all the principals to address the information he collected. In the spring, he then planned to visit each secondary school again to see how they were managing to implement the possible changes generated from the fall visits and the national conference. We were headed for one of those return visits.

Bill, his wife Caroline, an educator from Lesotho, our driver, and I reached Molimo Nthuse Lodge after a visit to Maseru. Only a seasoned and expert driver could have negotiated the one lane mountain road that brought us here. A look out the car window revealed a perilous drop should the car veer even a few feet to the left. Furthermore, any car coming the other way had no choice but to backup for miles, because there were no lay-byes.

I never did figure out what rule determined who backed up when, but I didn't care. I wasn't driving, nor directing the driver. I didn't have to be sure we were going the right way, or quietly pray in the back seat that the driver was truly headed for the destination I requested. I didn't have to make the reservations at this lodge, nor, more accurately, ask some hotel operator to make them. I was ensconced here in this comfortable lodge, where I didn't have to navigate anything on my own, and most of all I was with people I knew.

My current relaxation stood in major contrast to my tension a month ago when I was making my way down the Arab souk in Jerusalem like a running back with a football, dodging blockers, heading for my goal line of a youth hostel. The blockers turned out to be young Arab men stepping in front of me asking incessantly, "You American? You American?" My London Fog trench coat and Dansk suitcases on a luggage wheel rack broadcast "tourist" louder than a bullhorn.

I foolishly answered the first of these queries with, "Yes. Why?" Whereupon I was pulled vigorously into one of the markets to sample its wares. Extricating myself from the stall, I continued to progress slowly down the souk, while I ignored the constant barrage as best I could. I felt harassed, unprotected, and alone. Shaking with fear about what might happen next, I barely held it together as I dragged my luggage slowly over the cobblestones.

Upon hearing, "You American?" again, I just surrendered. Thinking to myself, I don't care if I am murdered, raped, or whatever, I have to stop. I turned into the nearest cafe and collapsed into a chair.

The owner, a comfortably oversized Arab man with grey hair, sauntered over to my table and suggested I might like a cup of mint tea.

"Yes, please."

He left to fetch it and returned with a smile as he placed a small cup in front of me. "I think you will enjoy this."

After I took a sip of the sweet fragrant brew, I managed to sigh out, "Thank you."

"May I ask where you are headed?"

"I'm looking for the Lutheran Hostel, but can't seem to find it." And I certainly wasn't going to stop and ask anyone, I thought to myself.

I had chosen this hostel on the recommendation of an American math professor I met at a Tel Aviv hotel before crossing the desert into Jerusalem. We had dinner together the last night I was there. After exchanging the usual pleasantries, I confessed that I found staying in strange hotels in foreign countries a lonely business.

"You should try hostels; they're much more friendly and it's easier to meet people."

After our dinner, I headed for the front desk, called the Lutheran Hostel in Jerusalem, and made a reservation there for the next two nights.

While I sipped my thick, mint tea, the Arab man spoke again, "The Lutheran Hostel is nearby. After you have relaxed with your tea, I'll call my nephew to guide you there."

Within 15 minutes I was checked into a simple, clean room. After a quick lie-down before dinner, I washed up and headed downstairs with a mental picture of conversing with a group of folks around a table instead of entering a hotel dining room to sit alone.

A beautiful hymn arose as I walked through the door of a high-ceilinged room. I recognized the tune, but not the words. Ahead of me lay a multitude of tables with about six to eight folks at each one. I found an empty space at one of them, slipping into a chair just before grace commenced. The cadence felt familiar, but words seemed to be in a foreign language. When grace was over and folks began to converse, I realized it was a foreign language. Everyone spoke German.

I sighed silently at the loss of the anticipated comfort of company for conversation over dinner. A growing sense of futility stole into my heart and took up residence. I began to consider changing my itinerary. Instead of heading for India after I reached South Africa, perhaps I'd return to London. Surely Connie would be glad to see me.

Only later could I chuckle at this quiet joke of the universe. I made a few efforts to converse that night with one or two folks who spoke minimal English, but our conversation came to naught. (Their ability to speak English well surpassed my knowledge of German, which didn't even include the knowledge of how to say hello.)

As we arose from the table after dinner, a woman nearby approached me, introduced herself as Helga and said, "I invite you to come to Masada with me tomorrow."

I didn't know what she was talking about, but the name Masada sounded familiar; she seemed most pleasant and happily could speak English.

"Yes, that would be lovely. How will we get there?"

"By bus."

And so began a fascinating day forever fixed in my memory. The next morning we boarded a bus together. By now I'd grown accustomed to the Israeli soldiers standing guard on every bus. They looked younger than my kids, but seemed comfortable with a gun slung over their shoulders. Two hours later, we were exploring the ancient fortifications of Masada perched high on a plateau overlooking the Dead Sea where Herod the Great once took up residence. The desolation of the plateau called up what I learned later was the mass suicide of the Sicarii rebels in the siege of Masada during the first Jewish-Roman War.

While my stay at the Lutheran Hostel didn't yield the warm conversation I sought with fellow travelers, it did bring me a companion for a day's journey to an historic site and reduced my intense longing for the supportive connections friends, family, and colleagues.

By the time Bill and I left the riverbed, the sun had come up. Although our fingers were covered with glints of gold, we were empty handed and still quite happy. After breakfast, our full car headed for the St. James mission in the mountains of Lesotho.

Traveling with Bill and Carolyn, I relaxed for the first time in months. In this carefree state, I could truly absorb and appreciate the stunning beauty of this high kingdom located in the northwest corner of South Africa. The dark clouds of loneliness lifted—burnt away by Lesotho's brilliant sunshine and the comforting support of familiar folk. While my trip to Masada had begun to pierce my feelings of despair, only the presence of long term friends and acquaintances could provide the uplifting break that gave me the resolve to continue onto India instead of returning to London.

HOW TO DEVELOP SUPPORTIVE CONNECTIONS

Man is by nature a social animal.
-Aristotle

One of the critical threads of your self-care cocoon includes those supportive connections (friends, family and colleagues) who appreciate, respect, and encourage you. These are the folks you count on to back you up—the people who make you laugh, who challenge you, and who celebrate your accomplishments with you. No one person can provide all these joyful additions to your life; you need a posse to nurture your mind and soul. And, of course, you in turn, nurture theirs just by being you.

Supportive connections bring some surprising benefits in addition to the immediate joy of hanging out with kindred spirits. Strong relationships with friends, family, and others actually boost the immune system and lead to a longer life. DAY 3 is devoted to helping you consider and build those connections.

Friends

Who are your local friends? Like many of my midlife clients, you may be neglecting one group of this cohort—your gal pals. Remember Selena who wanted to reenter the job market now that her two kids were in school all day? In addition to adding a new job and a running regime to her life, she also craved the company of her friends on a more regular basis. With her step-to-it style, she decided to set up a mother/daughter book group that would meet at a different house each month. She relished the company this book group provided and when her turn came to host, she loved collaborating with her daughter to choose the book for the month and the dessert to serve the group.

Or perhaps knitting/sewing/crocheting/weaving occupies your time. I'm a member of a local Stitch and Bitch group that brightens my day once a week. You could start one, or join a group at a local yarn store, or community center.

Where are your far-away friends? In one of our early coaching sessions, Kara said to me, "I want to focus on friends and fun more. I've been so invested in my career and my writing; plus Tom and I have been so busy raising Todd, I've neglected my oldest friends. It's been more than three years since we've met for one of our long weekends together. I miss them. Now that Todd's going off to college, I'm going to organize a spa getaway for us. I need it; we need it!" Kara named this group her "Girl Gang".

If Kara's hankering resonates for you, why not contact those old friends of yours? Her plan of gathering at a get-away spot removes everyone from the daily chores of cooking and cleaning. A spa weekend may not fit into your life right now, but a simple phone call to say hello to an old friend, or a conference call with your girl gang might just put some spring back in your step and theirs too. Whatever works for you is always perfect.

Colleagues

Do you have colleagues at work? Colleagues provide that automatic companionship of folks you see almost every day, or in weekly meetings. You naturally enjoy some colleagues more than others, but regardless of your feelings, all these folks provide a stabilizing social network for your everyday life. This kind of support is not the same as your friendships. While you may form friendships at work, they can fray when work structure or power plays interfere. Everyone needs friends outside the workplace; they can also make great sounding boards for your work concerns.

Even with the company of colleagues, the workplace can leave you feeling oddly lonely. This was the case for Joan, a corporate vice-president working in Chicago. In a quiet conversation one evening, she lamented that she often felt lonely in her "testosterone-driven" workplace, and, further, there was no one she could talk with about her dilemma. As a division head in a large corporation, her equals were all male and viewed their jobs and themselves "very differently".

I easily sympathized with her situation, because I faced a similar one in my job as Dean of Continuing Education at Wellesley College. Unlike Joan, my daily companionship needs were more than met on the job. I simply loved my daily work of mentoring and advising the return-to-college students at Wellesley; I enjoyed greeting my staff every day as I entered the Continuing Education House and especially valued my weekly meetings with the other class deans. But there was no one on campus who faced the specific joys and challenges of advising older students, who were a minority on campus. While the other deans were wonderfully helpful when dealing with students' academic concerns, I felt isolated when working with other issues their students didn't face such as child care, campus parking, elder care, and divorce—to name just a few.

I was to benefit from a piece of serendipity in this regard. At the end of my first year as dean, I attended a two-week residential program on life-long learning at the Harvard Graduate School of Education. The program proved to be both educationally useful and immediately practical. However, conversations with my roommate yielded the biggest benefit. She worked in a similar program at Smith College. By the end of those two weeks, we hatched a plan for working together and supporting each other. In a year, she, her boss (the director of the Smith program), and I, along with others, created a consortium called CENTS (Consortium for the Education of Non-Traditional Students), which involved all the big and little Ivies that featured programs like Wellesley's.

I no longer felt isolated. In my next 18 years at Wellesley, we met once a year at a different college for three days to hash over problems common to all of us. If you feel lonely at work, consider the possibility of creating a group where you can bring your concerns to folks who face similar issues. These gatherings could significantly enhance everyone's work, provide solutions to everyone's particular dilemmas and even help prevent all members from making unnecessary mistakes. CENTS certainly provided all that for me. It makes such a difference to be able to go through things together.

Could you take a class? The return-to-college students I advised at Wellesley always enjoyed the company of other students who were in a similar position. Over lunch, they could talk about the common challenges of finding child care, taking care of parents, or juggling the demands of work, school and family.

Taking a class in a subject of particular interest can create new connections for you. As a break from the pressured daily routine of her corporate culture, Joan opted to take a landscape photography class. She soon found herself looking forward to joining the other class members as they captured different local scenes. She also found this venture called forth some creative talents that had lain dormant.

Do you volunteer? Many women find themselves volunteering in their communities—often in service to their children's schools. The connections you form during volunteer work are much the same as those on the job—some are supportive and some are not.

Marjorie created a welcome connection for herself when she was asked to be a room mother for her son's third grade classroom. She agreed to take on this responsibility if she could share it with another mother of her choice. With this condition accepted, she grabbed her cell to call her friend Sharon. She remembered the time when the two of them ran the library bake sale and doubled earnings of the previous year. Along with this smashing success, their friendship grew, as did the fun they had together. So

Marjorie's heart beat a little faster when she heard Sharon say yes to her request as she imagined the good times they would have in the coming year.

The next time you decide to contribute to your community as a volunteer, consider Marjorie's approach. How can you make this volunteer work support you? Perhaps you love the work involved, or the people involved, or the cause, itself. For example, books cast a magical spell on Marjorie at a very early age, so she delighted in the opportunity to support her son's school library. Since Sharon spent her days baking all kinds of goodies for her girls, they proved to be the perfect team to run the library book and bake sale event. Or if you love to garden, you could seek out a garden club, or perhaps help to create a community garden.

Folks in Your Community

Sometimes supportive connections arrive in the daily acts of living. As you're walking past the produce aisle of the supermarket, maybe the manager says hello to you with a big smile. Or when you stop into your local coffee shop, the barista starts your usual "large latte with whole milk, no sugar" before you reach the counter. Or the owner of your local knit shop sits down with a bemused smile to puzzle out where you have gone awry on that Irish fisherman's sweater you started a few weeks ago.

When I lived in London that Fall, I came to know the butcher and the green grocer around the corner in my daily rounds of shopping for food. Their welcoming smiles helped ground me in this new territory. Regular hellos from your pharmacist and shopkeepers in your neighborhood can provide a daily lift you may not even recognize until, like me, you are propelled into a foreign land where everyone is a stranger.

Now that I live in Rhode Island where there are more farms per person than any other state, I head for the Coastal Market—a local organic farmer's market—every Saturday with a friend. In addition to obtaining wonderfully fresh organic food, we love the opportunity to support our local farmers and the connections we form with them at this market where "everybody knows your name".

Family

> *Maturity is doing what you want to do,*
> *even when your mother thinks it's a good idea.*
> – Paul Watzlawick

How do you connect with your family of origin? Families come in all shapes and sizes with different benefits and meaning for each of its members. You may derive great satisfaction and nourishment from your family, and/or your family relationships may be a bit more complicated.

Everyone is imprinted in early life with patterns ("defenses" if you want to use a psychological term) that serve you well when you are younger, but may not be useful as you age—especially when you find yourself stuck at the midlife crossroads. Two quotes reveal this truth. The first came from a friend who sighed one day to say, "Your parents are your final exam." And the second from spiritual leader, Ram

Dass, "If you think you're enlightened, go spend a week with your family."

When you become aware of these no longer useful patterns, you grow and evolve, diminishing the charge you may experience during family visits.

Who is in your current family? Perhaps the most powerful connection of all lies with your immediate family. As a mom, I focused my primary efforts on caring for my children as they grew. While I knew my love for them was unbounded, I wasn't consciously aware of how very much I would miss their daily presence. My own unconscious sense of a future living in an empty house with echoing walls probably sparked my own midlife voyage around the world.

When your immediate family structure changes, your life can turn upside down. An emptying nest or divorce often serves as a trigger for a midlife crisis. This strong reaction demonstrates the critical nature of the bonds with your immediate family.

While on my journey, letters from my parents and friends sustained me along the way. But most of all, reading letters from my sons that awaited me at every American Express port of call gave me a lifeline of sheer joy.

Pets

If you own an animal, you might believe that pets should have been included in the family section. For some owners, bonds formed with pets are as strong as those with humans—and far less complicated.

Pets can make you laugh with their antics, or relieve stress when you arrive home to your dog's vigorous tail-wag greeting or as your cat settles into your lap and purrs to your pats.

You may be a dog fanatic like my friend, Eleanor, whose second marriage created a household of six dogs, two of them hers, three of them her husband's, and then one adorable, dog-pound orphan they couldn't resist adopting.

Or you may hanker for more exotic creatures, like Karen who maintains a huge aquarium that holds two turtles, or Susan, with her pet boa constrictor. Or, you may lean towards the more traditional with a cat or two to keep you company.

Whatever pet or pets you own, they provide a supportive connection for you.

Books

Books support us in our solitude and keep us from being a burden to ourselves.

– Jeremy Collier

On my round-the-world midlife journey, I always made sure I carried a book in my bag. My travels took me into strange lands peopled with foreigners. I missed my family, my friends, and my colleagues to a degree I never anticipated. When I curled up with a good book, some of my anguish abated, as I got lost in the story. I suspect that the sadness you sometimes feel when you finish reading a great book is the loss of the temporary companionship the book provided.

Remember Marjorie who ran the library bake sale with her friend Sharon? Once she downloaded books with her library app, she grabbed her tablet whenever she took off for a doctor's appointment, so she could read her latest book while waiting. She often referred to her orthopedist as a one-book doctor, because she could almost finish a book in his waiting room.

TAKE ACTION

Are you ready to begin beefing up those supportive connections that provide such personal nourishment?

1. Start or join a book club that meets your wishes. Mother/daughter? Coed? Non-fiction? Mysteries only?

2. If you're a knitter, join a group at your local knit shop, or start one of your own.

3. Plan a get-away with some old friends who are spread across the country or world. Gathering at a get-away spot removes everyone from the daily chores of cooking and cleaning. Or if a spa weekend does not fit into your life, a simple phone call to say hello to an old friend, or a conference call with your girl gang might just put some spring back in your step, and theirs too.

4. Gather together a group of folks who have similar workplace concerns. These gatherings could significantly enhance everyone's work, provide solutions to everyone's

particular dilemmas, and even help to prevent all members from making unnecessary mistakes.

5. If you're a stay-at-home mom, or work out of your home, gather a group of women who may face similar issues for weekly, biweekly, or monthly meetings.

6. Check out local classes to find one of interest to you that meets at a convenient time, then sign up for it. What subject sounds like fun? Photography? Literature? Ethics? Science?

7. Volunteer for an event, or join a club that calls on your talents and interests. For example, if you love to garden, you could seek out a garden club, or perhaps help to create a community garden.

8. Plan a family event this year that's new and different. Could be simple—brunch together if you live close by, or an adventure in the city visiting a museum after lunch, or at a spa day together.

9. If the idea of a pet is calling you, head for your local animal shelter and adopt a dog or a cat. Be sure to stock up on the appropriate food first. This is a big one—enjoy!

10. Stick a paperback in the trunk of your car, or download a good read from the library onto your tablet, so you will have a companion ready for that wait in the doctor's office, or waiting to pick up a child at school. Don't forget to appreciate the company a great book can supply.

Which action did you choose to implement?

I am willing to implement # __________

Now TAKE ACTION!

DAY 4: Optimal Organization

Delhi, India – March 1981

In March, I found myself in Delhi hankering to explore the old city. After a morning of work, I headed for Connaught Circus and strolled by the columned shops of the circle. While gazing in the window of one shop, I heard the wheel-like sound of roller skates behind me. Turning quickly to get out of the way, I spotted an older man with no legs perched on an early version of a skateboard. With only hands to propel him forward, he moved with astonishing speed. Aiming right at me, he uttered, "Baksheesh, baksheesh" over and over. I ran; he followed—moving closer and closer until I escaped onto bumpier pavement that slowed him down.

While baksheesh literally means a tip for service, the most common definition I encountered on the streets of Delhi was "give please". I learned rather painfully that if I handed a few rupees to a child who looked especially needy, a swarm of children and adults encircled me with hands out ready to receive, murmuring "baksheesh, baksheesh".

Moving through a crowd of beggars with my head down to escape eye contact proved to be an excruciating challenge. My temporary solution was to stop giving. While this resolution left me feeling slightly safer on the streets, it also burdened me with regret.

After this Connaught Circus roller-blade chase, I returned to my simple room dripping with sweat and exhausted. A refrain from an old Noel Coward song we sang around Connie's piano bubbled up in my mind, "Mad dogs and Englishmen go out in the midday sun"—to which I added, "plus one very naive American." I figured this particular lyric probably derived from the experience of the colonial Brits in India.

That evening, when the last of the heat dissipated and I could concentrate more easily, I reviewed my options for the near future. The day after tomorrow, I would head to Srinagar for a three-day stay on a houseboat on Dal Lake to view the grandeur of the Himalayas. After that, my plans for travel in India remained unclear until I flew to Sri Lanka in nine days. With my Air India ticket in hand, I could travel anywhere in this country, so long as I did not return to the same place twice. Where to go?

Perhaps it was the evening cool, perhaps it was the empty space in my plans, or perhaps it was simply curiosity, but on a whim I decided to call Vasanthai Pai's deputy, Captain Narsingh the next morning.

I met Mrs. Pai a year earlier at Brandeis University, where a friend and colleague asked me to join a weekly study group on Special Education at the Heller School. One morning, as we sat around a table discussing a controversial Supreme Court case, the leader of our group welcomed a visitor from India, Mrs. Vasanthai Pai. As Director of the Federation for the Welfare of the Mentally Retarded, a privately funded organization in India, she spoke eloquently about her organization's efforts on behalf of the children there.

When our meeting was over, Mrs. Pai and I talked informally, and I disclosed my plans to be in India the following March. On hearing this information, she broke into a big smile, took my name and address, and enthusiastically exclaimed she would make arrangements for my visit there. Later I received a letter from her outlining the possibility of different speaking engagements in India with the name and telephone number of her deputy in Delhi, Captain Narsingh. She promised to write again when the speaking plans and arrangements for my stay were firm. Regretfully, no letter arrived before I left for Paris in January.

My shoulders dropped in disappointment when I remembered her promise, because she seemed so positive about her plans for me when I came to Delhi. Despite this lack of follow up, I decided to call Captain Narsingh the next morning. His welcoming response caught me by surprise.

"Oh, Dr. Leonard, I'm delighted to hear from you! In three days you will be speaking on mental retardation to the annual convention of the National Institute of Mental Health in Bangalore. You will spend the night there as a guest of Vallai and Tamil. The next morning Dr. and Mrs. Pai will drive you to Mangalore and then the following day you will head for the Medical College in Manipal, where you will address doctors and medical students on the diagnosis of learning disabilities. After spending the night, they will return you to Valli and Tamil's house in Bangalore."

How wonderful! Evidently Mrs. Pai's letter outlining these plans arrived after I left and did not get forwarded. But now my plans were set. How comforting to have this structure in place.

But, how daunting! I knew little about mental retardation; my specialty was learning disabilities with a focus on diagnostic work. What in the world could I say about mental retardation to the thousands of people attending the convention? There was no possibility of doing any research to prepare—especially on a houseboat in the Himalayas before the advent of the Internet.

Somehow, the strangeness of the world around me lessened my anxiety. This challenge was just one more on a trip where confronting the unusual was my daily routine. I had no expectations for what might happen next, or how people might behave, and I had no control over the environment around me.

Perhaps this openness mandated by traveling in foreign lands allowed a seminal idea to pop into my head. I remembered that the mothers of retarded kids in the U.S. had advocated strongly for equal educational opportunities for their children. Their efforts led first to the enactment of a state law in Massachusetts (Chapter 766) and then to a Federal Law (94-142, The Education of All Handicapped Children Act)—based in part on the Massachusetts law. Since I helped write the regulations for implementing the Massachusetts law, I knew quite a bit about it.

Days later in Bangalore at the National Institute of Mental Health conference, this law and its history provided the theme for my presentation. That focus—along with a lively and lengthy Q & A period—rendered my talk a resounding success. (In fact, the hosts asked if I would be willing to meet for a session with their doctoral psychology residents when I returned to Bangalore a few days later.)

After speaking with the doctors in Manipal, my car ride back to Bangalore with Dr. and Mrs. Pai provided a life-altering moment. Seated comfortably in the back seat, images of our recent travel together danced through my mind as we drove along. That morning after breakfast before my talk, they took me to the ocean saying, "We know how much you Americans like the beach." Later that afternoon on the road from Manipal to Mangalore, they pulled into a small market, so I could buy something for myself. The moonstone bracelet I purchased there for a ridiculously low price still brings happy memories of that day every time I wear it.

We also stopped at a classic temple of a goddess devoted to women who are awaiting the birth of a child. Four-year-old girls with heads shaved to honor the goddess frolicked on the grass outside the temple. As we entered the gateway to the temple, a blast of warm, moist air filled with unfamiliar and intoxicating scents assailed me. My eyes caught the flickering movement of colors beyond the palate of my Western eyes while my ears filled with song and for the first time I experienced the exotic dancers, music, and incense that characterize the temples in the south of India.

Rolling along in the back seat of the car, I recalled all the thoughtfulness and care of this powerful couple in the front seat. I sighed quietly and I pondered how I could ever repay these extraordinary hosts. They would probably never come to the U.S. again, where I might extend some hospitality. As a mom on her own with an academic's salary and two kids in college, I couldn't make a meaningful donation to the Pai's Federation. What could I possibly do? Hindsight tells me that perhaps giving a presentation to thousands, along with a prepared lecture to doctors and medical students, plus an afternoon spent with that year's psychology residents might have provided some exchange for all their largess. But I sat there with guilt washing through my veins.

Finally I spoke. "How am I ever going to repay you for all your kindness?"

Laughter erupted in the front seat from both of them. Finally Dr. Pai turned to explain what had tickled them, "You don't pay us back; you pass it along to others." Long before the expression emerged in the U.S. popular culture, I learned in that moment to "pay it forward"—a truly life-changing gift. For years thereafter, any time I spoke with a student in my office and lightened her load in some way, I knew I was following the Pai's advice to pass along the kindnesses you receive.

HOW TO DEVELOP OPTIMAL ORGANIZATION

The quiet and capable organization of Dr. and Mrs. Pai along with Captain Narsingh shaped a wonderful adventure for me, which included a special life-changing moment. And that is the true benefit of organizing your time—to free you up for greater things than trying to remember what you are supposed to do and where you are supposed to be. Liberated from remembering these details, your productivity improves along with a sense of achievement and mastery. When you move more easily throughout the day, your stress level lowers, so you have time to appreciate those special moments.

A good organizational system should also grant you a feeling of control over your life, at least over those events you can control—no promises about hurricanes, traffic jams, or other people's bad moods. A good system yields this result by organizing, tracking, and reviewing the bits of information you carry around in your head. Each one of these bits requires a decision to be made, or action to be taken.

When unaddressed, all these unmade decisions and incomplete actions divert your attention unconsciously, depleting your energy stores and leaving you feeling overwhelmed and out of control. Once you move the decisions and needed actions out of your head and onto a page, computer, or mobile device, they no longer demand your subconscious attention. You feel more in control and have extra energy freed up to accomplish those big dreams of yours.

So let's develop a tailor-made plan just for you on Day 3 of your self-care journey, by learning how to select, set up, and run a time management system (TMS) personalized for you and your life.

Maybe you already organize your time and tasks with ease; if so, simply skim this chapter for a few ideas to tweak your system. Or perhaps you've been looking for a better TMS and can upgrade your current setup, so you free up time to address the powerful changes midlife brings. Or, if you've thrown up your hands in despair over finding a good scheme for yourself, today you can begin to trade in your present TMS for a new, improved model.

Or maybe you believe you do not need and would never use any TMS. Actually, you do; we all manage our daily and yearly to-dos with some kind of system. For example, you might make long lists, post stickies around your space, post a family calendar on the fridge, or keep those doctors' appointments in a stack on your desk. Whatever system you employ, you can enhance it today.

Are You More Like Fran or Judy

Your organizational nature is the first step for designing the right system. Running a TMS may be second nature for you. It was for Fran, a woman I met at a conference one April. She dazzled me with her efficient and effective approach to life. She appeared sublimely content, as she outlined her morning ritual of exercise, shower, dressing, and personal writing. She accomplished all these activities in the same sequence by 7:30 every morning, when she sat down to enjoy a healthy breakfast before work. My eyes popped as she described how she set her alarm for 5:45 am to start this early morning regime.

Fran found her system so powerful she couldn't understand why everyone didn't operate in the same way. Clearly, she thrived on this linear approach, with tasks all confidently sequenced and reviewed on her iPhone. I observed she was not managing a household of kids, but I'll bet she would still operate in the same linear fashion if she did.

Judy, a former coaching client of mine with four kids, displayed a very different temperament from Fran's. Fran's regime would have increased Judy's stress level, because she preferred to head where her spirit moved her moment by moment. She completed the tasks she assigned herself, but used a more spiral approach, cycling back to a task rather than completing it all at once.

At Judy's request, I once coached her on improving her time management skills. At the time she felt exceedingly frustrated and confused because she had two systems: one in a small, black, six-ring notebook and the other on her computer. She didn't like either one and balked at the regimentation of any TMS—even though she knew she needed one. As we worked together, she decided to keep her TMS in the small, six-ring notebook and do away with the one on her computer. This decision worked well for Judy, because locating all your lists and information in one accessible place is key to an effective time management system.

Judy also made her black, six-ring binder system more personal by decorating her pages with drawings and pictures. She spent a good 15 minutes on the phone with me detailing exactly how this new system would look and feel. When I checked back with her in a month to determine if this new setup worked for her, she happily described how she was organizing her days to great effect according to the blueprint we created.

Develop the System That Works for You

A little analysis will lead you to discover just the right TMS. Be sure to fashion it for yourself the way Judy did. Take the time to focus on every detail of what you truly desire. I'm not suggesting you spend so much time on this exploration that you never take the next steps of setting up your system and taking it out for a test drive.

To begin, ask yourself a few questions. Do you want a small, easily portable book, or do you want a computerized system for your mobile device? If you want a book, do you want your pages a week at a time, or a page for each day?

Do you like space for each hour? Where do you want to put your to-do, to-call, or to-text, to-email lists? What color do you want the cover to be? Want your book zipped or latched?

Or if you prefer a mobile device, do you like the calendar app that came with it, or do you want to adapt it? Do you want to find a different time management app? What color cover do you want for your device?

Trust Your Inner Seven Year Old

One of the craziest and most useful things I learned at a time management workshop years ago was that it's the seven-year-old child inside you who gets the job done, so tap her talents when you design your system. For example, Judy's seven year old loved different colors, so she purchased colored highlighters, so she could highlight completed tasks. This approach worked beautifully for her, but might leave your seven year old bored or annoyed.

You can also count on the fact that your inner-seven-year-old's moods and tastes will change. Judy initially added bug stickers to her binder, but later found her seven-year-old self was bored by the praying mantises, ladybugs, and caterpillars, and wanted flowers. Judy obliged her.

The Basic Components of Your TMS

Since you will locate all your information and lists in one accessible place (a big time saver), let's review the basic components you need.

Your personal information: Be sure to enter your name, email addresses, phone numbers, fax number, etc. In this way, if you lose your planner or device, the possibility exists you may retrieve it. If you use a device, be sure the "locate this device" is set up. For security's sake, you may want to keep a separate list of your passwords in a small notebook by your computer.

Your yearly overview calendar: This includes the months of the current year and future years at a glance. These are great for planning purposes, when you need to calculate how far way a future event will be.

Your daily pages: These comprise the heart of your TMS on your device or planner where you will record your appointments and events months in advance. (Yoga class every Tuesday evening, doctor's appointments, etc.) The beauty of recording these events weeks or months ahead of time is that you only enter them once. Efficiency is what we are after here. Once you ensure that these calendar basics are a part of your TMS, you can then proceed to develop the final component: the ever-so-useful Information Bank.

Your information bank: This provides one-stop shopping for all the data you need at your fingertips. Here are some suggestions for sections you might want to include.

- *Your address directory* This component is a necessity—complete with email addresses, phone numbers, streets, cities, zip codes, fax numbers, etc.

- *Family and Friends* with information on their birthdays and anniversaries, which can also be integrated with your yearly and daily calendar.

- *Books, Movies and Music* is where you can note recommendations from sources you respect. For example, Fran showed me how she used the Notes app on her iPad to record all the books she read, so she would not download one she had already read from the library.

- *Meetings* can provide a space for preparing agendas and taking notes at meetings.

- *Projects* allow you to list and track ongoing projects. Fran used *Numbers* (Apple's version of Excel) on her iPhone for tracking projects.

- *Desires* is for your "someday/maybe" list. Be sure to review it regularly and add to it upon occasion.

- *Travel* enables you to record information about upcoming trips, frequent flier numbers, packing lists, etc. Judy found her pre-trip stress level dropped dramatically when she developed a permanent checklist for what to do before a trip (stop mail, water plants, turn down heat, etc.) and another one for packing basics (tickets, sunglasses, prescriptions, suntan lotion, etc.)

- *Financial* makes it easier to track expenses. Again Fran uses her *Numbers* app for this process.

- *Ideas* will encourage you to note those moments of inspiration, so you can remember them.

Why not observe yourself during the next week and notice just what kind of information you want to access every day? In that way, the sections you add will be tailored especially for your own life.

Setting Up Your TMS

Once you have selected your TMS and begun to customize it, you are ready to prepare it for operation. The easiest way to start is by filling in your Address Directory. (If you already have a complete Address Directory, you can move onto completing another section in your Information Bank.) Since this kind of entry is a repetitive task with no immediate reward, I suggest you add some entertainment. Try completing a chunk each night as you watch a TV show that does not require your undivided attention. Judy actually found it meditative to enter her addresses during the day while she sat on her deck, watching the birds at her bird feeder. After your Address Directory starts to fill, you can take on the challenge of reducing that midlife brain overload.

How to Get That Stuff out of Your Head and into Your TMS

The first step to clearing that brain fog is to list all of the things on your mind right now that require an action or a decision. This process is amazingly useful. I invite you to try it. Take out a sheet of paper, hop onto your computer, or grab that tablet or phone and list everything on your plate right now—yes, all those things you have been meaning to get to. To help get you started, you can focus on your physical spaces, your personal relationships, and your future plans.

Your desk:	What needs doing there?
Your home:	Maintenance needs?
Your closets:	Easily accessible?
	With clothes you like to wear?
Your family:	Birthdays coming up?
Your friends:	Any you haven't seen in a while?
You:	What are your dreams for yourself?
Travel:	Upcoming trips?
	Travel plans?
Financial:	Expenses you need to track?
Ideas:	Any inspirational thoughts of late?

This "brain dump" is the first step to setting up an effective TMS. It may be one of the most useful methods of clearing your mind ever discovered. With your brain dump list in hand, you can move forward with four steps.

Step 1: Review your brain dump, marking each item with
YES—will do it,
SOMEDAY/MAYBE, or
NO—never gonna do it.

Step 2: Delete or cross off all the NO items. This surprisingly beneficial activity ensures these thoughts are now out of your head. The fog is lifting.

Step 3: Enter the SOMEDAY/MAYBE items in a section of your Information Bank, so you can review them from time to time.

Step 4: Now take your YES items and schedule them into your TMS, even if they are weeks or months away. This list of items comprises the heart of your system and needs to be comprehensive.

When you get your system up and running, your life will be calmer if you repeat this process in a way that works for you. A weekly, monthly, or seasonal brain dump, followed by these four steps will seriously reduce any "overload anxiety". As you schedule your YES items into your TMS you can also determine if there is enough to time in the day to do what's in your list. If not, time for some cutting, but more about that later.

Lucinda, a former coaching client and freelance journalist told me, "I always carry my monthly calendar with me noting everything I need to do—days articles are due, work appointments, my children's schedule, time for just my husband and me to be alone, and quiet time for solitude and prayer. Even though I'm incredibly busy, I follow the schedule for both work and play."

Marcia, a single mom with two sons, and a return-to-college student at Wellesley College, described the benefits of her TMS endeavors, "I decided to make an actual schedule of all my activities including household duties, work, class time, lunches, dinner, time with the kids, everything, including blocking out study time. The more I keep to my schedule, the smoother things go for me."

Start With Small Steps

When you move your YES items off your brain dump list and into your TMS, I recommend that you chuck them down into small steps. Specifically, what will it take to accomplish your goal? For example, if "reading assignments for course" is on your YES list, the steps might be:

- Check out and locate assignments and their due dates.
- Chunk down and schedule in TMS.
- Complete reading according to schedule.

This example may sound a bit exaggerated, but you may want to check out the assignments at the beginning of the course, and then chunk them down and schedule them when you have time a few days later. You'll conduct the reading, itself, throughout the length of the course.

This chunking approach is particularly appropriate for assignments if you're in school or simply taking a course. When I worked at as a dean at Wellesley, I noticed that new students tended to schedule large blocks of time for reading a single text, The human brain is wired for variety, so take advantage of that fact and schedule diversity into your activities.

Put Yourself First

A tendency I have noticed among many women is that they schedule their own needs last. This may not be true for you, but it is for many women. Midlife presents a perfect time to reverse this order in your universe. As Sonia, a wise client once advised, "Give time to yourself before everything, everyone else. Your time will be more valuable to others when it is coming from a strong, healthy place. Often, I can feel crabby and rundown if I do not do something for myself."

When you find yourself in one of those crabby moods, do a mini brain dump with your own well-being as the focus, and then complete one item on that list before you do anything else—even if you simply sit down for a minute or two and take three deep breaths.

Operating Your TMS

Be prepared. You can actually expand your work time with some clever planning. Lisa who has a full time job and growing family says, "I never waste a minute. I bring my tablet with me everywhere, for jotting down notes/ideas, reading books and articles, and sometimes catching up on email. I carry it to doctors' appointments. Yesterday I had to wait one solid hour to see a breast surgeon, but was able to work the whole time because Wi-Fi was available in the waiting room. I also always take an hour to do something I love every day—knitting, reading, writing." Gerry, a former student says, "The best advice I could give anyone about how to manage her time is to use each moment to the fullest by carrying a piece of assigned reading wherever you go. There are always moments when you have to wait—for a bus, for an appointment. Always have a book or an article with you so you can spend time reading."

Remember that any plan is better than no plan. Planning reaps bountiful personal rewards. When you devote time to reviewing and updating your TMS, your life flows with greater ease. If you are a person like Fran, who benefits from routine, schedule this survey activity at the same time every day. As she notes, "I make a list every night and then I prioritize it for the next day." Or if, like Judy, you prefer a more casual approach, update your planner every day when the spirit moves you.

Why not take advantage of having all the components of your life located in one convenient spot? If you are reading a book or musing as you load the dishwasher, and suddenly an idea pops up, or you remember a to-do, you can stop what you are doing at that moment and enter it into your TMS.

With a small amount of planning effort, you can obtain surprisingly big results because you will be moving that "stuff" out of your mind and into your TMS. You will feel more in control of your life, and your mind will feel less burdened. Remember this will free up more energy and time for pursuing those big dreams of yours.

Setting priorities can be tricky. So what happens after your brain dump if you have more items on your YES list than you have time for in your schedule?

The tried and true solution to this problem is to rank order your list the way Fran does. Schedule your top priorities first; put the others on your SOMEDAY/MAYBE list, or even in the trash. Sounds easy. But what if you have to chose between a favorite activity and doing research on paper, for example? Depends, if you are a student and the paper is due soon, you will probably head for the library or the Internet and postpone that favorite activity of yours. But do keep a wary eye on this process, because if you always postpone those activities that restore your energy reserves and give you joy, you miss out on much of what makes life worth living.

I remember one student at Wellesley who came to see me because her teen-aged daughter had been hospitalized repeatedly in the last month. Jan had devoted every available moment to seeing that her daughter was situated in a residential placement where she couldn't hurt herself. Jan was also trying to finish a final paper for a course and needed a further extension on a deadline already extended by the Academic Review Board.

I had the discretion to grant this extension, which I did. I could see Jan was dealing well with an extremely challenging circumstance and believed she would be able to finish the paper in the extra time allotted. But my advice to her at the time was to take a day off from everything. Her stress level was in the danger zone. I worried that if she postponed time for herself much longer, she might become physically ill with no prospect of completing her paper by the new deadline.

Practice saying NO. Whenever you set priorities and postpone—or remove—items from your list, you are saying NO to something or someone. In Jan's case she risked saying NO to finishing her final paper, when she attended to her daughter.

Jan's situation, however, is not typical of your day-to-day experience of setting priorities. Most moms would say YES to a child's compelling need, but in your daily routine, learning to say NO to those activities that do not advance your agenda can be a challenge. You may find it harder to say NO to someone than something (coffee with a friend versus cleaning out the refrigerator), but it is a skill you can learn. On Day 7: Time on Your Terms, we'll explore some strategies to help you improve your NO saying.

TAKE ACTION

Ready to bolster your skill of Optimal Organization? Cast your eyes over the possible action steps below and pick one. If you've never tried a brain dump, I suggest action step 3. You might just find it one of the most useful methods for clearing your mind you ever encountered.

1. Determine where your TMS will be located. Computer/tablet/phone? Binder? Sounds pretty simple, but if you begin to locate all your "stuff" in one place, your daily life will improve.
2. Decorate your TMS home. Stickers? Magic markers? Home screen and lock screen wallpaper? Will you use photos? Include animals, seasons, kids, flowers? Remember that seven-year-old who needs attention!
3. Perform the brain dump outlined in the how-to section and enter the results in your TMS. This activity will take a bit more time than some of the others, but will bring substantial rewards.

4. Check to be sure there is breathing time scheduled between each of the events in your TMS. If not, reschedule one to create that time.

5. Take one action outlined in your TMS that only requires 10 minutes. (You might check out assignments and due dates for a course.)

6. Pick an action totally devoted to your own well being and implement it. (If you don't have one listed in your TMS, then add one!)

7. Review your daily plans for the rest of the week.

8. Install a library app on your tablet/phone. If you already have one, download a book. Or borrow a book you'd love to read from your local library.

9. Add one item into your TMS that would be especially fun for you. Yes, just plain fun!

10. Design an activity to improve your TMS and implement it. Who knows better than you what will work best?

Which action did you select for today?

#__________

Now TAKE ACTION!

DAY 5: Nurturing Environment

Bangalore, India – March 1981

I made my way down the lighted stone path toward the guesthouse—my temporary abode in Bangalore. After easing into the soft cushions of the couch in the living room, I reviewed the delicacies of the enchanting meal I just enjoyed with Vallai and her family. Who knew fried banana flowers could taste so delicious? Or that eating off a palm leaf with your fingers could be so easy and so much fun? Or that a hostess would be thoughtful enough to include some less spicy dishes for a guest with Western sensibilities?

I sank deeper into the soft couch cushions, relishing the nurturing environment provided by this hospitable family.

My contentment that evening stood in remarkable contrast to my feelings a month earlier while standing at the reception desk of the Hotel Concorde in Cairo as I heard the words.

"Madam, there is no room available."

"But I made reservations at this desk a week ago," I cried in a strained voice trying to regain my calm.

"I'm sorry. There is no room."

"What can I do?" I pictured myself alone on the dark streets outside.

"I will call other hotels to locate a room. I cannot promise success; it is a busy week in Cairo. May I suggest dinner?"

Dinner was the last thing on my mind, although I had been eager to return to the friendly dining room of this hotel with its revolving world-travelers always eager to share a meal. Good company and good food beckoned, so I headed to the elevator and pushed the button for the second floor where white tablecloths, sparkling crystal and animated faces greeted me as I stepped off. Sure enough, a man in front of me in line swiveled around to ask if I would like to join him for dinner.

Turned out he was a salesman from Belgium. Sales appeared to be the primary occupation of this hotel's residents. I never met anyone like myself at the Concorde—a professor on sabbatical. Or, more personally—a divorced mom, who recently sent her younger son off to college.

My dinner companion, Emile, proved to be both affable and informative. When I described my hotel room dilemma, he patiently explained I had ignored an important part of hotel etiquette in Egypt by neglecting to give the desk clerk a thank-you present.

"You mean a bribe?"

"No, no, it must not appear to be a bribe. You bestow it nonchalantly."

"What should I give?"

"Oh, chocolates, cigarettes, wine," he replied with a Gallic shrug.

I stored away this bit of information, and after dinner headed reluctantly back to the desk. A hotel room had been located. Hallelujah! A cab had been called to take me to this new hotel along with Monique.

"Monique?" Evidently another woman ousted from the Concorde would ride with me. We entered the taxi on the street, as she chattered away in a most charming French accent. A seasoned traveler at the age of 26, she appeared unruffled at this turn of events, having just returned from Chad.

To my profound relief, the desk clerk at the next hotel was expecting us and introduced Jafari who would show us to our room. "Our room?" My heart flip-flopped; I was to share a room with a complete stranger. We trailed after Jafari, who opened the door to a small room with a big problem. There was only one bed. It was not king-sized, nor queen-sized; it was simply a double mattress on a box spring on the floor. I lost it. Collapsing into the room's only chair, I started sobbing.

"Vat is zees?" demanded Monique at the sight of my tears. "Zees is nozzing!" she admonished. "In Chad, I eat ants!" Then, more gently, "Come, we go to zee bar; you feel better."

And go to the bar we did. We met two delightful companions: a Frenchman my age, who couldn't speak English and an American her age who couldn't speak French. She spent the evening chatting in French with the older man, and I had the pleasure of talking in English with a kind, young American who reminded me of home.

While listening to this talkative lad, my loneliness lifted. A lyric from *My Melancholy Baby* floated through my mind and I chuckled silently when I heard the words, "every cloud must have a silver lining." I was indeed a melancholy baby who found unexpected sunshine in a strange hotel bar in Cairo.

I even found an opportunity to administer a "bribe" the next day when I returned to the Hotel Concorde. I had left one suitcase there, since I preferred to wait for my midnight cab to the Cairo airport in the lobby of a familiar hotel.

With a newly purchased carton of Marlboros, I approached the desk clerk, thanked him for holding my luggage overnight and gingerly handed him a carton of cigarettes.

"Oh, but I couldn't accept this."

"Please take it," I replied—nonchalantly, I hoped.

"I cannot."

This isn't going well, I thought to myself with a rising sense of ineptitude. I had no idea of what to do with an extra carton of cigarettes, because I'd given up smoking years ago. Disappointed at my lack of success, I grumbled, "Then I'll have to throw them away; I don't smoke."

"Oh! In that case, I will keep them. Thank you!"

That pack of cigarettes delivered a potent punch. My hours of waiting in the lobby were filled with service of the finest kind, including offers of snacks, whiskey, soft drinks, and discounts at the gift shop. When my taxi finally arrived, the desk clerk personally escorted me out the door, tucked me into the cab, and waved a heartfelt good-bye. I collapsed into the back seat—simply spent from worrying about whether I could locate a bed for the night and the moment-by-moment stress of trying to find one.

After this experience and many others like it, resting at the guesthouse in Bangalore provided remarkable relief from the daily pressure of ensuring my basic needs were met.

Tomorrow I would leave India and regretfully wave good-bye to Vallai and her hospitable domain here in Bangalore. Thanks to her nurturing environment, I felt restored and ready for whatever awaited me when my plane touched down in yet another foreign land.

With this thought, my eyes closed and my head tipped back gently onto the couch pillow.

HOW TO CREATE A NURTURING ENVIRONMENT

> *You must have chaos within you to birth a dancing star.*
>
> – Friedrich Nietzsche

Chaos shadows every true metamorphosis. When a new form arises, the old form is destroyed. Before the caterpillar turns into a butterfly, it dissolves into gelatinous goo within the chrysalis. As your familiar world begins to fade at midlife and a new one has yet to emerge, chaos may be your companion.

One reader of my *Midlife Discovery* newsletter described her muddled feelings this way, "I can actually feel it in my head when my thinking is undergoing major change, like white noise." Another wrote, "After 25 years in public education, I am limping down the last two years to the finish line. I feel like the pretty party balloons have all gone flat and are lying around the ground being blown about aimlessly."

When your own life begins to shift in anticipated ways (emptying nest), or when an unexpected event induces change (restructured out of a job), like the caterpillar, you can create a protective chrysalis for your own internal restructuring. On DAY 5 of your Self-Care journey, you'll learn how to build this nurturing environment for yourself the way Vallai did for me, to protect the profound internal transformation that can characterize this period of life.

How to create such an environment? Since the world around you consists of things, places and people, you can build your own supportive structure by focusing on these three arenas.

Things

Why not start when you're relaxing at home on your couch or chair? Take a moment to pause and look around the room sensing your feelings about what you see. As you examine each item, ask yourself, "Do I love it? Am I happy it's here?" If your answer is "Yes," that's great; enjoy it! If your answer is "No," time to clear what has now become clutter. What if you don't love it any more, but it's still useful—like a lamp? Keep it; you may want to consider buying a new lamp, but that's a job for another day.

Or, if you prefer, you can start with one of your clothes closets. Simply go through your wardrobe and pull out any item you haven't worn in the last two years. (Experts usually suggest one year, but two years makes it easier to say good-bye.) If this approach leaves you uninspired, here's another method. Instead of plowing through your clothes to find items you haven't worn in two years, start by taking all of your clothes out of the closet and lay them on your bed. This time, examine them one by one to locate the items you love, adore, and want to keep—what you would buy today. Now place these lovable clothes back in your closet.

A coaching client of mine named Sarah haltingly confessed one week that she had not made any changes to her house since her husband died more than a year ago. With a big sigh, she agreed to my weekly request to start clearing out her former husband's closet. I knew what courage this would take and understood her comment that those clothes allowed her to believe her husband was still here in some way. But I also suspected she might be ready to say goodbye to them, because she, herself, brought up the issue as bothersome to her.

The next week, Sarah described how she had cleaned out his closet, piled all the clothes into her car and driven the whole lot to the Salvation Army. She initially considered giving some of her husband's clothes away to her nephews, but realized the quickest route was the best one for her. I could hear the energy rise in her voice as she related the story of her accomplishment.

Months later, Sarah went on to sell her house in the suburbs and move to a condo in the city so she could spend less time taking care of her large house and gardens and more time going to museums and the theatre. Clearing out one closet started this journey to discovering who she had become at this time in her life.

If your time is too limited to go through a closet, one of those overloaded kitchen drawers is probably begging you to cast an eye on its contents and dig out the utensils you never use. If you wish, dump out the drawer, finger through its contents, and locate those utensils you actually use regularly and return them to the drawer.

Once you locate all those things (clothes, household items, etc.) that no longer serve you, your next step is to remove this clutter from your life. Simply bundle up a pile of those no-longer-needed household items or clothes. Then give them away to a charity, bring them to a consignment shop, or use any approach that works for you.

This kind of clearing brings immediate benefits. First of all, you learn more about the woman you have become and what she wants. For example, perhaps you're tired of those neutrally colored clothes and crave more exciting hues in your life. Or maybe you're weary of all those loud, bright colors and seek a more neutral and peaceful palette. Good to know!

Another reward for clearing this clutter from your life is that sense of relief and that surge of energy that arrives right after you let go of objects, which no longer reflect who you truly are right now. So if you're yearning for something new to arrive, start clearing! You can absolutely count on that law of physics, "Nature abhors a vacuum."

Places

When you clear the clutter out of your home, you naturally improve your living spaces. However, when you look around and see the difference your clearing made, you may realize the colors in your rooms no longer please you. Just as you might discover a desire for brighter clothing when you gaze at your closet, you may also find a preference for a particular color in the spaces around you—peach, for example. By all means, honor this wish. It reflects the new, emerging you. Paper a bathroom, or paint a wall, or buy a throw, or pick out pillows that reflect that perfect shade of peach for this transition time. Then step back and admire the changes you wrought.

Why not consider the spaces where you spend your days and update them to reflect the woman you are becoming? You may not be able to describe her yet, but you know what she likes and what she doesn't, what fascinates her and what bores her. While you may have less control over your office at work, you can still make changes that dramatically affect the emotional feel of your workspace. A large wall hanging of embroidered elephants, for example, portrays a different atmosphere from a bold graphic print. Find those elements that scream, "That's me."

Penny craved an update for her house especially now that her youngest child was headed off to college. With college tuitions reining in family finances, she had limited funds to spend, but with her children gone, she had some more time to play with.

One Saturday morning, she gave the "sit-on-your-couch-decide-then-clear" exercise a try in her living room. She was rewarded with a lighter, brighter space. This result inspired Penny to head for the paint store to select three pale yellow paint samples for the walls. She chose one, which went beautifully with her white woodwork. On the following weekend, she finished painting her living room and felt as sunny as her newly painted walls.

You can also locate nurturing spaces outside your home or work. Why not consider heading for those locations that just plain nurture your soul. For some women, a visit to a museum provides a relaxing and nourishing way to spend some time. A stroll through the galleries might leave you full of wonder and joy.

For many folks, any spot in nature soothes away the cares of daily living, and even the bigger ones of life. By all means head for the beach, put your toes in soft, white sand, and listen to the restful sound of waves lapping the shore. Or take a hike in the mountains, sniff the intoxicating scent of pine, and feel the refreshment of cooler air as you climb higher and higher. Or go for a simple walk in some nearby woods and listen to the crunch of leaves, or feel the dirt path beneath your feet.

People

When enmeshed in this midlife metamorphosis, you may also notice that spending time with certain friends and acquaintances doesn't nourish you in the same way. Maybe your monthly ladies luncheon group begins to feel more like a chore than a rewarding experience.

Or perhaps you long for more company rather than less companionship at this stage of your life. Why not locate a local book group, or start a regular gathering of kindred spirits around an interest of yours. As I mentioned, I head for my weekly Stitch and Bitch group every Thursday.

Are you simply yearning for different companions? It's OK if you do not find the same kind, happy energy in your exchanges with some of your friends and acquaintances. No need to blame anyone here—including yourself—or to try to fix the other person, or remedy the situation. As Sonia Sotomayor recently noted in an interview on Book TV, "If you fix this, things will be better—what a useless conversation!"

There is no need to do anything other than watch your own internal responses and release any charged feelings. Some friendships and groups may fade and others may grow as you let old patterns go and bring in new approaches to living. By all means, honor every one of those feelings during this transitional period.

TAKE ACTION

Time for your action step today! Was there an idea in the last few pages that especially resonated with you? Take a look at the possibilities below and choose your favorite. Or make up your own.

Whatever you select, be sure to implement it today and keep moving on it tomorrow. For example, maybe you pick #1. "Sit on a couch or chair in your living room, look around, determine what you love and mark each item that needs to leave in some way with a sticky note. Tomorrow you can continue this exercise by removing those items you did not love. Perhaps you pile them in the trunk of your car to take to the Morgan Memorial. On the following day you might drop them off. In other words, you go step by easy step until the job is complete. So let's go!

Which one calls to you?

1. Sit on a couch or chair in your living room, look around, and determine what you love and what you don't love. Mark each item that needs to leave in some way with a sticky note.

2. Head for your clothes closet and remove every piece of clothing you haven't worn in years.

3. Or how about that kitchen drawer that may be full to the brim? Open it up and pluck out those items you haven't used in years.

4. Take a walk through the rooms of your living space and muse about color you might like to remove or add. What would it be? Perhaps all is harmonious and feels just right, Great! You know the colors in your living spaces are perfect for where you are in your life right now. The appraisal, itself, counts as an action step.

5. Or as you walk through your spaces, pause to wonder if there is an item you would like to add to your environment—a new lamp, a framed photo of a favorite spot, two of those pillows you spotted in a catalog the other day?

6. What about the color of the walls in one room? Would you like a change? Head for the paint store, or wallpaper emporium and bring home some samples to see which pleases you the most.

7. Find an exhibit at a local gallery or museum and make specific plans for a visit—not someday maybe; make a definite date!

8. Locate a specific spot in nature (mountains, beach, etc.) that feeds your soul. Head there today or make plans to go on a specific day at a specific time.

9. Think of a nearby location (a park around the corner or a hammock under a tree in the back yard) you can easily access. Open your front door and head there.

10. Create your own action step to implement today. As you ponder the things, places, and people in your life, how might you create a more nurturing environment for yourself.

Which action did you choose to implement?

____

Now TAKE ACTION!

DAY 6: Time on Your Terms

Kuala Lumpur – May 1981

"You headed for Penang tomorrow? They have most beautiful sunsets in the world there," blurted Jing-Wei—a pint-sized, energetic woman who lived up to the meaning of her Chinese name, "small bird".

She sat across from me in a lively circle of men and women engaged in high-spirited conversation at a restaurant in Kuala Lumpur. I was enjoying this most entertaining group over lunch thanks to my host Armand.

I met him a little more than a year ago back in Cambridge, Massachusetts when I attended an event organized by the Kennedy School's Visiting Fellows at Harvard—thanks to an invitation from one of the Fellow's wives. Armand encouraged me to contact him when I arrived in Kuala Lumpur on my upcoming sabbatical, which is how I found myself lunching with this charming group.

At the party in Cambridge, Armand sported the casual clothes of that era—jeans and a green polo shirt. By contrast, when he arrived to take me to lunch in Kuala Lumpur, he wore a white T-shirt and a long, blue batik sarong—perfect for the hot weather of the tropics.

While Jing Wei raved about the world famous sunsets in Penang over our delicious curry-filled meal, my heart beat a little faster. The next stop on my journey already beckoned powerfully. After busy days of travel and meetings in Singapore and Kuala Lumpur, I longed for some down time—a quiet pause by the ocean seemed a perfect antidote.

This yearning for respite echoed an earlier time when I hit the beach in Sri Lanka. After weeks of giving presentations and conducting interviews all over India, I found myself seaside on this other island for three days with an empty schedule. Instead of relishing a much-needed break as I sat on the beach with my toes buried in the sand, I shifted about—anxious and guilty because I wasn't working. I never soaked up the full nourishment of this leisurely intermission. I remained in my Western goal-settling mode despite my recent discovery of a totally different concept of time on an earlier visit with my hosts in Tanzania, Mary and Joseph Mungai.

Mary was the wife, who invited me to the Kennedy School's Visiting Fellows function courtesy of her husband, Joseph, a former Minister of Agriculture in Tanzania. Mary was pursuing a Master's Degree in Administration at the Lesley College Graduate School where I worked. At the social gathering that evening, she and Joseph generously encouraged me to stop at their home for a few days in Dar Es Salaam, while on my upcoming journey around the world.

During my visit there, one day after Mary and I explored Dar Es Salaam all afternoon, we returned to her home. As we walked through the front door, Mary noted, "Too bad we missed Cecilia."

"Who is Cecilia?" I inquired.

"She is a friend."

"Did you know she was coming?"

"Oh yes."

"We could have returned earlier." I responded apologetically.

"Oh no need, we were happily engaged."

I proceeded to ask further questions to determine if I had caused this seeming misadventure. I learned instead this present time orientation was a preferred approach in Tanzania.

In an "ah-ha" moment, I finally understood the African students who arrived at my office to see me without an appointment, and then waited patiently outside my office for an hour hoping to talk with me while I met with students who had scheduled appointments. I had encountered "African time"—the more leisurely, relaxed, less-rigorously scheduled, in-the-moment lifestyle, which contrasted remarkably with my tightly determined Western days.

Even after learning to appreciate this experience with African time, when I sat on the sand of a gorgeous Sri Lankan beach, I still reverted to my East Coast go-go-go attitude and simply bit my lip with worry.

By the time I reached Penang, however, I was ready to rest and recharge without an overly developed sense of responsibility sending waves of stress-inducing cortisol through my body. In Sri Lanka, my brain had been so busy spinning its guilt wheel, I could not truly appreciate the sustenance of that seaside spot, but when I reached Penang, the wheel simply stopped.

For two days, I relaxed on the beach, luxuriated in the warmth of the sun and allowed the soft warm breezes to soothe away all the cares and concerns of my journey. Grounded in mother earth, I tuned fully into my senses, which anchored me into the present moment.

This time, the toes I tucked under the sand were painted a particularly lovely shade of pink. I had located a nail salon and treated myself to a pedicure that decorated and soothed those feet that had taken me so far. I was rested and ready for the adventure that lay ahead, yet I flew away from this island of gorgeous sunsets with a certain trembling at the possibility of entering communist China (if I could only obtain a visa in Hong Kong).

HOW TO CREATE TIME ON YOUR TERMS

On DAY 4, you worked on developing a TMS (Time Management System) worthy of Captain Narsingh. Today you will enhance that system, so you can manage your time on your own terms and vastly improve your life every single day with a few simple steps that will break your chains to the world of shoulds.

Are you a Lark, an Owl or a Hummingbird

Remember Judy and Fran from DAY 4? Judy set to her allotted tasks as the spirit moved her, and Fran thrived on a regular routine and went running at exactly 6 am each weekday morning.

Judy and Fran initially designed their calendars with an awareness of their personalities. A knowledge of their individual body clocks helped them further refine their systems in ways that enabled them to live an even more contented life.

After listening to a pre-recorded segment of a Dr. Oz show on larks and owls one day, Fran discovered why it was relatively easy for her to rise at 5:45 am and hit the road by 6 am. She was a lark. Larks are those up-early (sometimes even before dawn), ready-to-roll folks.

As you might guess, Judy usually remained fast asleep when Fran was lacing up her running shoes. Judy always knew she was a night owl. In college she did most her studying past midnight in the dorm living room, while her lark roommate slept soundly in their dorm room.

Judy took advantage of her owlish ways when she went back to school at midlife to get a master's degree. Once dinner was over and her kids fell asleep, she pulled out her books and went to work. Breakfast was another matter. She could barely crawl out of bed in the morning to prepare this meal and get the kids off to school. Happily, her husband Mike took on this responsibility three days a week, so she could catch up on her sleep.

According to Smolensky and Lambert, out of 10 folks you know, two will be owls like Judy and one will be a lark like Fran. The rest will be "happy hummingbirds" likely with a predisposition toward the lark, or the owl.

What kind of bird are you—more of a lark like Fran, or an owl like Judy? If you're like Fran, by all means, schedule some heavy-duty activities on your to-do list in those early morning hours. But if you lean more to the owl end of the scale like Judy, nix the morning run idea, find a better time to exercise and use that productive late evening time in a way that works for you. If you are a hummingbird in the middle, your most productive time will probably be late morning

You may also find that you become more lark-like as you age. If you have teen-age children, you will recognize the truth of this finding! You may be aghast at how late they stay up at night and how much they like to sleep in the morning. One of my coaching clients learned her college-age son scheduled all of his college classes after noon, so he could sleep late. She also received the occasional middle of the night phone call from her son, who was genuinely surprised to learn she was asleep at 1 am.

Happily, you can take advantage of your own natural rhythms and operate your TMS for your lark, owl, or hummingbird temperament.

Think Like a Marine

Another way to enhance your system is to think like a Marine. One afternoon during a coaching call, a client named Moira lamented, "I'm shot; I'm on empty."

"Sounds like it's time to fill your tank," I replied.

In the years before I took this magical midlife journey where I rested for three days on the beach in Penang, I often felt just like Moira. After a day of working full time, going to graduate school full time and raising two teen-agers by myself at home, I often ran on empty.

Fortunately, my Dad arrived one January to teach me a lesson about "running on empty" when he flew north from Florida for a meeting in Boston. As was his custom, he took me out to dinner and asked how things were going, then listened patiently as I proceeded to describe the current challenges of my life.

When I stopped to take a breath, he said, "You need to build up your reserves; I learned that when I was in the Marine Corps. I never knew when I might get woken up at 4 am and ordered to march for 20 miles, so I needed to keep my tank full." The image of having to wake up for a 20-mile march resonated with me. While such a demand was never made of me, I recognized the feeling of being required to exert effort when I was running on empty. After that dinner with my dad, I became more conscious of ways to build up my reserves.

I scheduled a little breathing time between the tasks on my daily to-do list and curtailed my obligations a bit. If my office hours ended at 5 pm, I left work at 5 pm instead of hanging out an extra 10 minutes in case someone might stop by to see me. I also began to schedule two hours of what I called "reserve time" into my weekly schedule—just plain empty space with nothing to do.

While I occasionally slipped into exhaustion mode, I learned it was my job to be sure my tank was at least partly full—no one else could do it. Later, during my magical midlife voyage, I learned to truly fill my tank to the top with deep rest and relaxation when warranted.

You can make sure your tank is full, too. Whatever the state of your present life, why not build up your reserves with breathing space between tasks in your TMS? Eliminate any unnecessary tasks and then create some reserve time, or empty space, in your calendar because you will need that extra time. Your cat may get sick and need to be taken to the vet, your windshield wiper could break and require replacement, or a relative might be hospitalized and you will want to visit them.

What Fills You Up

Once you create it, what will you do with that reserve time in your calendar if no emergency pops up? Where will you be? Moira expressed such a concern when she asked me, "So what do I do with that empty space in my day?"

"Truth be told, I haven't the slightest idea, but you know!" I replied a bit cryptically. "Take a minute and think of all those activities that nurture your soul, that fill you up, Moira. Gardening? Taking a walk? Simply sitting quietly with a cup of tea, taking a quick nap or meditating for 10 minutes."

"Well, it sounds foolish, but I love to leaf through fashion magazines to see the latest styles and imagine how I might incorporate them into my wardrobe. I don't have a lot of extra money to spend on new clothes, but I can buy a scarf in a trendy color or an inexpensive piece of jewelry."

"Do you have plans to spend any time that way in the coming week?"

"Heavens no! I have more important things to do than leaf through magazines. As it is, I can barely stay on top of all I have to do."

I knew that with two kids, a husband with a full time job, and a full-time job herself, Moira had more than enough on her plate, but I also knew that if she classified activities that filled her up as luxuries and dismissed them, she was on the royal road to burnout.

So I posed a question, "What would it look like if you scheduled a half an hour a day for simple luxuries like leafing through a fashion magazine?"

"Wow! That would amazing!"

"Could you?"

"Well yes! I usually eat at my desk to catch up on email, but I could take my lunch to the local coffee shop, grab some chai tea, and forget work for a half an hour."

"Would you be willing to do that on two days next week?" (As a coach, I usually give my clients a request at the end of each weekly session, which they can accept, refuse, or counter offer.)

"Sure!"

A week later Moira reported she found her energy actually increased when she carved a half an hour out of her day for lunch and perused magazines instead of munching on her sandwich distractedly while answering email.

So what fills you up? Like Moira, you may be surprised to discover small luxuries that cost little in time or money.

Bust Your Stress with These Navy Seal Techniques

For another way to upgrade your TMS, head for a different branch of the Armed Services. Research on the training of Navy Seals provides four fine ideas for dealing with stress. In those stress-filled moments, you live under the rule of the cortisol rushing through your body. Reducing stress allows you to live a calmer and more successful life. I have Tom Hoobyar—a wonderful writer about NLP (Neurolinguistic

Programming) who is sadly no longer with us—to thank for being able to share this stress-busting knowledge. His blog about this research noted that despite the careful recruiting of prospects for the Navy Seals, 75% burned out with exhaustion after the initial weeks of training.

When the Navy explored the reasons for these failures, researchers discovered fitness and strength were not factors; rather, the candidates who dropped out could not control their instinctive reactions to stress and froze or folded in the face of seemingly overwhelming odds.

Based on this research, with a hope to keep more of their well-qualified candidates, the Navy developed a program to develop "mental toughness." After implementing it, the Navy SEAL pass rate for the initial training increased by over one-third. What worked for the SEALs can work for you and you don't have to become a SEAL to learn the four techniques the Navy discovered to increase performance under stressful conditions.

Set goals. This first approach requires you to put your attention on how you are going to get through the next half-hour rather than thinking about the rest of your life, or even the rest of your day. This kind of close-focused goal setting is a key to peak performance anywhere. It doesn't matter whether you're facing an audience of 1000, discovering you forgot to pack that lunch for your son's school picnic, or awakening to the sounds of a crying child—you can beat this stress by narrowing your focus to the immediate future.

Visualize. You probably know that Olympic athletes use visualization to increase their athletic performance. You can too by rehearsing the successful completion of an event over and over—i.e. you see it, you hear it and you feel it. For example, perhaps anxiety haunts you about that upcoming presentation to 1000 people. You might see yourself easily mounting the steps to the stage, feel yourself speaking confidently to this large audience, and hear a happy round of applause when you finish. Each time you rehearse this event you can add more sensory cues. Notice how your body feels and the sounds you hear and even what you smell. As you do this again and again, your brain experiences success each time.

Change your self talk. You will remember the concept of self talk from DAY 1: Self Compassion. Hopefully by now you are observing your negative commentary, calling a halt to it, and reframing it into a more positive remark. If you accomplish only one task during this week, reversing your negative self talk into a personal cheering section might lead to the most positive change in your life.

Control your arousal. You can use this technique to quiet the physical symptoms of a panic attack, when you feel overwhelming anxiety and your heart pounds or you break out into a cold sweat, or for even those slightly anxious moments. While these reactions are useful when facing a wild animal, they do not help when you are asking for a raise. Some deliberate breathing can help you.

Inhale with a deep belly breath for a count of six; hold your breath for a count of two; then exhale for a count of six, emptying your lungs. Do this three times. You can practice this breathing technique anytime during the day for immediate stress busting.

By putting these four techniques into action, you will diminish those anxiety-inducing moments that arise every day and be able to spend time on your own terms rather than in the control of an aroused brain.

TAKE ACTION

Are you ready to take action so you can spend the days of your life in a state of being and behaving that totally suits you? Choose one of the following action steps and hop to it today.

1. Decide if you are a lark, an owl, or a hummingbird. Then make one change in your schedule today to reflect that knowledge.

2. Eliminate one unnecessary item from your schedule for the upcoming week.

3. List 10 things that relax your mind and restore your soul. Then pick one to implement now, or to schedule it into your TMS.

4. Look at the year ahead and conjure up a way to spend a day or two that would provide you with deep rest and rejuvenation. Set aside this day, or two in your TMS to insure it occurs.

5. List three goals you hope to accomplish, but you never seem to get to. Select one and schedule the first step into your TMS.

6. As the day goes by, the instant you find yourself in a slightly stressful moment, focus only on what you need to accomplish in the next half hour.

7. Choose an upcoming event that causes you anxiety as you think about it. Practice visualizing it in successful terms. Rehearse it, being sure to call up positive sensations over and over.

8. Monitor your self talk for the rest of the day, calling a halt to any demeaning comments like, "you idiot". Reframe them into the kind of words you would hear from a cheer-leader.

9. Watch yourself during the rest of the day to see when you begin to panic, even a little. For example, a car suddenly cuts in front of you as you're driving down the highway. Practice your deliberate breathing exercise three times as you continue down the road.

10. Invent your own method for spending time on your own terms.

Which action did you decide to implement?

____

Now TAKE ACTION!

DAY 7: Completion/Celebration

Hong Kong – May 1981

The cab driver delivered the two other passengers to Hong Kong's luxurious Peninsula Hotel, then turned to me and asked again, "What address, hotel?"

"Ching Mi Hotel, 14 Hangkow Center," I repeated for the third time.

Two Aussies on a shared pony ride in the Himalayas suggested this place as one of the least expensive in Hong Kong. With my travel funds running low, I headed for this low cost residence where I could hang out for a week while I waited for a visa into China.

I didn't expect the Ching Mi Hotel to be fancy, but I bit my lip when the cab driver didn't recognize the name. After three more blocks, he threw up his hands and asked again, "Where, hotel?"

"Stop," I said, hopping out of the cab.

"Anyone here speak English?" I yelled to the stream of people walking along the sidewalk.

Two tall, young guys immediately hustled over.

"Do either of you know how to get to 14 Hangkow Center?"

"Sure, it's nearby."

"Would you come with me and direct the driver?"

They bounded into the cab and within three minutes the driver dropped us off in front a gritty enclosed square. The boys carried my two suitcases through the entrance to the square where an elevator to the left signaled the way up to Hotel Ching Mi. As one of them pushed the up button, I noted the sign above it which read, "Fire Hazard: use at your own risk."

The elevator stopped at the next floor, where my new companions kindly accompanied me to the check-in desk. A grimy desktop greeted us along with the smell of rancid fat. The cardboard tag on the key the clerk handed me was rumpled and brown with oil from the many hands that had used it before me.

"Can I buy you both a beer by way of saying thanks for getting me here?" I suggested to my companions

"No thanks," they replied quickly in unison.

"Well, please have a couple on me, and thank you again!" I said—handing them some Hong Kong dollars I hoped would buy two beers for each of them, as they departed with notable speed.

I grabbed my bags, headed for my room, put the key in the lock, and opened the door to the place that would be home for a week.

Oh boy! The smell of rancid fat now mixed with the light scent of garbage assailed me. This was far worse than I imagined.

But by now I had developed my "traveling legs". For months I'd been dogged by an almost existential fear of being on my own, in a strange home, in a foreign land. This fear had gradually faded and in its stead lived a far more resilient and resourceful self.

I turned right around and hastened down the hall to the front desk again.

"Do you have another room free?" I asked the desk clerk. "That one smells pretty bad."

"No, we don't. This might help." He reached under the counter to pull out a matchbox plus another small red and white box full of incense sticks.

I expressed my thanks and hurried back to the room to get the incense going.

After lighting a stick, and finding no chair, I lay down on the single bed to rest. Gazing up at the pink plastic walls, I noticed a bug crawling toward the ceiling—soon to be followed by another bug and another one, and another. Some were large, some medium-sized, and some small, but they were all the same bug. Yup, definitely cockroaches!

More than a little exhausted, I accepted these new roommates and lay watching them for a while. I figured the little ones were babies and the biggest ones grandparents. Years later, I read that the little ones were actually the oldest.

When my guides and I had rounded the corner to come into the covered square, I noticed a Best Western Hotel next door. I'll eat there, I decided. I can explore Hong Kong all day and only return to this room at 9 pm after enjoying dinner next door.

And that's what I did. I managed to sleep well every night to the wafting scent of some strong patchouli incense until one night, when loud music and ebullient voices woke me around 1 am.

Opening the door in my nightgown, I spied some guys, whom I later learned were from Nigeria, partying it up the end of the hall.

"Hey guys, please keep it down," I yelled. "I'm trying to get some sleep."

They laughed and turned to walk back into their room, then closed the door, which lowered the volume significantly.

I headed for bed again with a big grin on my face. I realized how far I had traveled—both physically and emotionally. Three months earlier I would have panicked the moment the cab driver couldn't locate my hotel; now I was yelling at strangers down the hall to pipe down.

San Francisco – June 1981

After a fascinating foray into China, an illuminating trip to Japan, plus a wonderfully restorative stop with my aunt and uncle in Hawaii, I headed back to the U.S. mainland. Leaning forward in my seat on the plane, I gazed out the window, hungrily absorbing every detail of the California coastline, then the city of San Francisco, and finally the airport runway as we touched down. In minutes, I would see my older son, Tim, who was working in California for the summer and planning to meet me. I had found my traveling legs on this amazing midlife journey, but I never stopped missing and worrying about my sons. They were wonderful correspondents. When I headed for the American Express office on entering a new country and retrieved my mail, it always included a letter from at least one of them to keep me in touch with their lives.

As I flew across the Pacific, I carried out my usual ritual to protect them. I pictured each son one at time, and gradually wrapped him in an imaginary golden thread until he was safe in this cocoon. This was a crazy exercise I developed to help calm my worried mind.

Bouncing on my toes while I waited to disembark from the plane, I hoped to spot Tim quickly in the assembled crowd. I should not have worried. There he was, looming over a large mass of people, smiling and relaxed. I wove my way through that crowd like a football running back. Almost squeaking with delight, I gave him a giant hug, as he said, "Welcome home, Mum."

He picked up my luggage and we headed for the Hotel California. At the registration counter, when I moved into my accustomed woman-traveling-alone-in-developing-country mode with queries and demands, my son put a calming hand on my shoulder, with the words, "You're home now, Mum."

I took a deep, satisfied breath, and a happy tear rolled down my cheek while a musical refrain, "Welcome to the Hotel California," rolled over in my mind.

After checking into the hotel with unaccustomed ease, we headed out the front door. Wide-awake after a long flight across the Pacific, I was raring to explore the city. Doing my best to catch up with Tim's long-legged stride, I marveled at the fact that I reached California for the first time, by traveling east instead of west.

Expecting to be shrouded by San Francisco fog, I was delighted when instead the city offered up a day of blue skies and brilliant sunshine for us to investigate historic Ghirardelli Square with its shops and waterfront dining, and other highlights of the city. With every step we took, I relished the sheer joy of being in my son's company and discovering the charms of this gorgeous city. I had found a perfect way to mark the end of an extraordinary midlife journey. My son was right; I was home… and ready to celebrate.

HOW TO DEVELOP COMPLETION/CELEBRATION

On this final day of your self-care journey you will engage the self-care skill of *Completion/Celebration.* I cobbled these two concepts together quite deliberately to encourage you to first recognize and then celebrate those times when you complete a project, a job, or a course of personal growth.

This natural conjunction of completion and celebration can be found in many important cultural rituals. For example, commencement ceremonies mark the successful culmination of four years of college or high school. Well known speakers, along with parents, relatives, and friends come from far and near to honor this important occasion. Sometimes students who excel in some way win special prizes, but every student who navigated those four years with passing grades receives a diploma to recognize this accomplishment.

Noting those completions that form a part of societal rituals is easy, but perceiving personal growth accomplishments is a far greater challenge. Before embarking on this midlife journey, my life was anchored in my family, in my home, in my friendships, and in my work. I lived every day surrounded by a familiar language and culture. These anchors grounded me and provided a feeling of safety, but I never realized they were there. Even when I lived in London during the first half of my travel, a familiar language and culture still supported me. And Connie provided the warm feeling of family and home.

During the second half of my trip, however, I unknowingly cast off these everyday moorings, traveling alone through unfamiliar territories day after day. When I could manage to enjoy the week I spent in that sleazy hotel room in Hong Kong with its generations of cockroaches, garbage smells, and noisy hotel guests, I had completed a successful inner journey. My smile upon returning to bed after quieting those noisy Nigerians down the hall signaled an awareness of that completion. The quiet happiness I felt at my ability to speak up was a personal win for me.

I had learned to live on my own in unfamiliar territory—a truly necessary accomplishment for the next phase of my life where I would be without the daily company of my sons. When I landed in San Francisco, I was aware of the physical distance I had travelled, but I was not aware of the inner journey I had completed and certainly never thought to celebrate that.

Fortunately for me, when my older son met me at the airport, celebration came naturally as we explored San Francisco together.

Definition of Completion/Celebration

This joyous end to a life-changing voyage occurred long before my days of becoming a life coach, but the lightness of my step as my son and I walked about this famous city suggests I was practicing the life coaching skill of *Celebration.* In a coach-training program I later attended, *Celebration* was defined as helping the client stop and fully recognize her achievement, whether it be a new awareness, or growth, or a more worldly accomplishment. Life coaches use *Celebration* to enable clients to deepen their appreciation for what they have accomplished.

When I first opened my practice as a life coach, I searched for opportunities to practice the coaching skill of *Celebration* and found them easily. But I noticed how often my clients skipped over their accomplishments—especially their personal growth wins—just the way I did. They seemed to ignore these achievements in a rush to move onto their next project, or even a new job. So I added "Completion" to "Celebration" to call attention to the completion aspect of this most important self-care skill of DAY 7.

Do you ever find yourself jumping onto the next task or project before even registering your past accomplishment? For example, have you considered how you might celebrate your completion of this seven-day journey? (Don't worry; we'll address that at the end of this chapter.) Or did you also think to applaud yourself for the simple change you implemented on the first day, or the second day, or the third?

Benefits

The good news about practicing this DAY 7 skill is you will be rewarded. When you celebrate your achievements, you bring a conscious focus to the positive moments of your life. With this kind of attention, you create more upbeat moments in your day. And who doesn't want more of that?

Furthermore, when you take time to acknowledge your own successes, they register consciously in your mind. If you want others to appreciate the results of your efforts, you must see them in yourself first.

Imagine if a child bolted through the door, excitedly telling you she was elected president of her class; would you ignore her comment? Give her no words of congratulations? Celebrate in no way? Probably not. It seems almost automatic to give a big hurrah on hearing such good news and plan a time to honor her success. Why not treat yourself the same way?

Would you like to work for an organization or department that never marked any milestones or achievements? A place where no one ever said, "We made it!" "We did it!" Celebrating accomplishments is motivating, so ask yourself what kind of internal organization you want to construct for yourself.

A person's inner work can be likened to climbing a mountain. In her book *Hands of Light*, Barbara Brennon notes that when you reach the top of the mountain (i.e. achieve a goal), the downward climb while you celebrate your achievement is critical before you scale the next mountain, or embark on that next project or job. You may not reach a greater height on your next climb if you do not undertake this downward journey of recognition and applause, which is what *Completion/Celebration* is all about.

Kaye Michelle, a colleague, once pointed to another benefit of this self-care skill in a conversation with me, when she described how positive acknowledgment of the onset of menstruation for a daughter can impact her. She suggested such recognition allows a young woman to "integrate the changes in her body and life as positive and gives her grace and confidence in the process." The cessation of menstruation is another time that warrants recognition for similar reasons. Many women take part in "Croning Ceremonies" to honor their entry into a "third age of wisdom." Marking any transition provides greater confidence when walking through a doorway into this new world.

Outer World Wins

How about you? Do you notice that once you complete a project or a job you move quickly on to the next one without so much as a by-your-leave to the work you just completed? When you achieve a big win, do you pause for a victory lap? If you are like most busy women, you probably don't.

When one of my clients, Joanie, found that new job she'd been seeking, she leapt into her new work with excitement and energy. As with any new job, she found the challenges engaging and sometimes exhausting. When I asked how she planned to celebrate landing this new job—a position she managed to obtain in a few months, while working full time, going to graduate school and caring for her family—she sounded surprised.

"How can I possibly find time to celebrate?"

"What could you actually do to honor this achievement?"

"Well, yesterday Tom reminded me I hadn't used the spa certificate he gave for my birthday."

"When might you be able to use it?"

"My friend Debby is coming to visit after Christmas. It might be a great time to do a spa day together."

"How does that sound to you?"

"Great, actually!"

"Are you willing to do that?"

"Yes," she replied with a giggle.

Inner World Gains

When immersed in your busy, day-to-day schedule, learning to acknowledge your personal growth gains can be even more challenging than honoring the more traditional gains.

Valerie comes to mind as an example. Remember Valerie from Day 1 who called me initially because she was so overwhelmed with her to-dos. To use her words, "My anxiety level is off the charts."

Using one of the action steps you encountered on DAY 4: Optimal Organization, (taking to-dos out of your mind and entering them into your TMS), Valerie developed a list of her projects, noting the tasks for each one, along with their deadlines on an Excel spreadsheet. Then she entered the tasks she expected to complete each week for the next three months. In a few weeks, her anxiety level dropped notably. Remember, if a task is taken out of your mind and written down, the specific worry attached to it is removed and your anxiety is naturally lowered.

However, when a new semester began, Valerie started feeling overwhelmed again and caught in the same anxiety trap. After a few queries from me, she realized that her feeling of discouragement actually signaled the great progress she had made. A "Yea for you!" helped her celebrate that advancement. She could acknowledge the distance she had traveled and recognize that improvement often occurs with two steps forward and one step back.

We also talked about marking this forward movement with a specific reward. Her packed schedule didn't permit any time-consuming event, so I asked if she would be willing to take a couple of mini-breaks during the day where she could celebrate little things like the completion of a successful class, or a feeling of calm, or whatever small progress she could observe in her inner or outer world. Valerie particularly loved an expensive brand of tea, which she decided to purchase for sipping to salute those small personal win moments.

The benefit of celebrating Valerie's accomplishments is that when I affirmed her achievements, she gained permission to praise and acknowledge herself. And you can, too.

TAKE ACTION

Now it's time to practice celebrating an inner or outer world win of yours on this final day of your seven day journey. Check out the actions steps below, chose the one that says, "Pick me" and go for it!

1. Determine a way to celebrate your completion of learning about today's self-care skill. What will it be? Now schedule it into your TMS—no"someday maybe" for this one.

2. Cast your mind over this past year of your life and find one achievement you can claim. Devise a plan to celebrate it and enter that into your TMS.

3. Look at the past year of your life for an inner world win. This exploration might be a bit challenging for you. Perhaps you notice you're breathing a little easier these days. Or smiling a bit more? Perhaps you are less judgmental of your own vulnerabilities. Be sure to note a time and place in your TMS to celebrate.

4. Keep your eye out for any small wins today and whenever you're aware of a small advance, find a way to honor it.

5. What's your favorite kind of tea, coffee, or other drink? Simply go online, or head for a local market and buy some. Then you will have it handy to celebrate a small moment of accomplishment during the day.

6. Create your own way to celebrate a life achievement either big or small. Be sure to enter the when and where in your TMS.

7. Maybe you've been struggling to find some personal inner or outer world wins to honor. I bet you have some successes from past years—ones you never celebrated.

Think of just one, write it down, and raise a glass to your achievement.

8. What about your family? What achievement could you all celebrate? Name it and then plan a way to honor it.

9. Design your own action step. Be creative on your own behalf.

10. Right now determine a simple way to let loose on completing seven days of acquiring self-care skills (dance around, listen to a favorite piece of music, meditate, spray a favored scent) and go do it! Be sure to return to read APPLAUSE TIME and discover a special reward to help you celebrate your completion of this program!

Which action did you choose on this final day of your self-care journey?

____

Now TAKE ACTION!

APPLAUSE TIME

Congratulations! You created a new regime of radical self care in only one week. You took action and developed a new self-care skill every day:

DAY 1: Self Compassion

DAY 2: Happy Body

DAY 3: Supportive Connections

DAY 4: Optimal Organization

DAY 5: Nurturing Environment

DAY 6: Time on Your Terms

DAY 7: Completion/Celebration

You actually carved out time and space for yourself in the midst of this crazy, busy, overwhelming world. I hope you can hear my hearty applause. Now take it in. Pause to acknowledge yourself for the work you accomplished along with the courage and persistence you displayed in reaching this critical goal of installing a solid self-care program.

But what if you're saying, I skipped a day or so and "only" introduced three new self-care skills to your daily life? Hold on! That's three ways you strengthened yourself so you can more easily meet the challenges of the road ahead.

Remember, you can always develop more skills if you like—next week, next month, or next year. But this week, you attended to your own needs in important ways. May I encourage you to simply "keep up the good work"?

You arrived at the end of this seven day journey while following me on my own midlife adventure around the world. Before I left, many friends suggested it was courageous for me to embark on this voyage. They were wrong. I did not fearlessly venture into the unknown. Rather, I naively set forth without considering the implications of a journey where I would find myself in unfamiliar places every day, where trees, houses, and people would all look different, where cars would drive on the "wrong" side of the road, where the cultural assumptions that guide my every day living would be unreliable and where—most disconcerting of all—being alone in strange places without family and friends would leave me lost and often scared. Far removed from the life I had known, without my daily roles of mother and professor, I felt unmoored, like I was nobody.

As I found my way around the planet in these unknown worlds, I bumped into the need to take care of myself while living on my own for the first time in my life. I learned more about the woman I was becoming at midlife and better ways to take care of her.

Toward the end of my journey, I became less fearful, and moved more easily into unknown experiences. I acquired a little more stoutheartedness. Years later, I realized my concern about an emptying nest was at its core a fear of entering uncharted lands.

Like me, you're probably traveling into unexplored territory since that is the nature of the midlife transition.

During this period, women go through a profound change in terms of body, mind, and emotions. What you have been doing for decades no longer works; it's time for something different. Yet, you cannot know what that will look like, because you have never been there before.

Such a daring transition requires that you strengthen the traveler by tending to her own needs first. As you worked your way through each day of this book, you began to administer this critical self care. The beauty of this program's design is that you can return to it again and again. When you feel like upping your self-care regimen, simply pick up this book, turn to a day of your choice and implement another one of the 10 actions listed at the end of the day.

With each action you will become stronger and more resilient as you move forward to create a life of greater meaning for yourself. And don't be surprised to discover that when you take better care of yourself, you will care for others more easily and thereby make the world a better place.

What's Next?

Now that you addressed that critical first step for navigating the midlife passage—i.e. strengthening the traveler—what's next? If you like, you can follow the next step I developed for women stuck at the midlife crossroads between "been there" and "now what?"

In my years of working with midlife women in transition as a Midlife Coach for Women and as the former Dean of Continuing Education at Wellesley College, I discovered that the secret to a more fulfilling life lies within you. I also found that guided journaling provides an effective way to access that inner wisdom. Based on these insights, I created a nine-week journaling eCourse called, *Reinvent Your Life ~ Write Now*. By writing your way through this program you will learn what you need for the journey, who you really are, and what you truly want for the years ahead.

Happy traveling!

Dear Reader,

Thank you for joining me on my travels around the world while you established your own self-care regime in seven transforming days. I hope the new system you developed will provide a solid foundation for success as you move forward to reinvent your life.

If you appreciated *Midlife Magic* and have a minute to spare, I would welcome a short review on the page or site where you bought the book. Your assistance in spreading the word is greatly appreciated. Reviews from readers like you will help other midlife women find a way to focus on their own needs and institute a personal self-care regimen.

Thank you!
Bonnie

Bonnie Leonard, EdD, CLC
www.bonnieleonard.com

Acknowledgments

Midlife Magic owes enormous thanks to

– the clients and former students whose midlife journeys illuminate each chapter.

– the generous hosts and kind strangers who gave me nourishment and companionship as I circumnavigated the globe.

– Lisa Tener, whose book-writing classes and structural editing prowess moved *Midlife Magic* from embryonic idea to reality.

– Nate Leonard, who gave his time and prodigious copyediting skills to improve each page of this manuscript. Any technical flaws that remain are my responsibility.

– Dawn and Steven Porter of Stillwater River Publications for the ever-present talent and enthusiasm they brought to publishing *Midlife Magic*.

– the folks in my book-writing course with Lisa and in the writing groups we formed later for their helpful feedback and assistance.

– my Wickford *Stitch and Bitch* friends for their weekly support and friendship.

– my Ingerdinner group buddies whose love and cooking skills are boundless.

– the Wellesley classmates whose encouragement is always there.

– my other friends, who lightened my book-writing journey.

– my family (my sons, their wives, and my grandchildren) who always keep my heart happy with their laughter, life and love.

About the Author

As a midlife transition coach for women and the former Dean of Continuing Education at Wellesley College, Bonnie Leonard, EdD, CLC has devoted her career to empowering women. With her guidance and mentoring, thousands of clients and students have found a successful route forward to reinvent their lives.

Awarded an official citation by the Massachusetts State Senate for her work at Wellesley College, Bonnie has appeared on *Good Morning America* and was recently featured in *The New York Times.*

Bonnie's own midlife reassessment propelled her on a sabbatical adventure, where she traveled around the world, solo—supported in part by the *Mary Elvira Stevens Traveling Fellowship* from Wellesley College. This journey impacted her life in profound ways and generated the motivation and ideas for this book along with her years of experience as a life coach and dean.

Formerly an Associate Professor in the Graduate School at Lesley University, where she led its International Studies Program, she holds a BA from Wellesley College, and an MEd and EdD from Boston University.

Further information about Bonnie, her life coaching services, and her online journaling course is available at www.bonnieleonard.com. She can also be reached at coach@bonnieleonard.com.

Made in the USA
Middletown, DE
04 December 2018